THE GOD WHO LOVED STORIES

OLIVER TREANOR

The God
who loved stories

How to enjoy reading Scripture

ST PAULS

ST PAULS Publishing
Morpeth Terrace, London SW1P 1EP, UK

Copyright © Oliver Treanor 1999

ISBN 085439 571 7

Set by TuKan, High Wycombe
Produced in the EC
Printed by Interprint Ltd., Marsa, Malta

ST PAULS is an activity of the priests and brothers
of the Society of St Paul who proclaim the Gospel
through the media of social communication

Contents

1

God the Storyteller

veryone loves stories. That's why soap operas on television score consistently high ratings. Why too book sales bring in big profits for novelists every year, and why the best of classic storytelling passes into the realm of literature that endures and is read over and over again.

The reason stories are important is they help us think about our experiences in such a way as to discover a meaningful pattern behind them. We follow characters in a narrative and recognize ourselves in them. We watch how they handle events and observe the outcome. Instinctively we are even exploring deeper questions such as, 'What is life about?', 'Why should I expect certain standards of other people?', 'Is there a point in being true to myself in the way I behave and react?'

The stories that attract children deal with such questions implicitly. They listen avidly because they are just beginning to live and have a lot to find out. Adults listen with no less interest because the questions raised by good stories are so basic they always require a more complete answer as life goes by.

Whether we realise it or not we are constantly searching for the purpose of everything – the world about us, the changes that time brings, our very existence, our inevitable death. You don't need to be a philosopher to wonder, you need only be human. The stories we tell somehow enable even the simplest among us to tackle the most complex areas of thought in a simple way.

Since this is true, it is no surprise to find that God used

the medium of story to speak to us in the beginning about himself and that since then he has never stopped creating stories that also tell us about ourselves.

The Bible is a library of fascinating tales. Although it contains many types of writing – law, poetry, visions, history, letters – it is as a narrative drama that it comes to life best. Real-life tales, fables, parables, myths, folklore, whodunits, romance, grand epics, personal confessions, sensational love-affairs, court-room dramas – they are all there in bright Technicolor. Like the best in storytelling they are designed to entertain as well as to instruct, to absorb the reader to make him read on.

Someone once said that God created us because he loves stories, and that we tell stories because we love God. There's a lot of truth in that. God's love for his creatures is the starting-point of every story. Had he not created us in the first place there would be no story to tell. Had he not redeemed us there would be no story worth telling.

By sending his Son to be a character in our saga God wrote the greatest story ever told. It is one we narrate over and over wherever the gospel is read, in our community prayer, at the Mass, in the celebration of the sacraments, in each one's personal history of growth in faith.

We tell God's story with our lives. Some tell it well; some tell it badly. When we take care with the part we play – how we deliver our lines and act out our role – God listens to his story in us like a child who yearns for the happy ending. Our story is essentially an interpretation of his. By letting us take part in the theatre of life, he allows us to enter into his stories and become part of his great idea for the world. By following his text as well as we can we enter into the drama we call salvation.

But let's begin at the beginning. The first tale that scripture unfolds is the magnificent legend of Creation. It sparkles in its simplicity and beauty – telling how God stilled the chaos of the dark void, separated the waters from the land, emblazoned the firmament with the sun and moon and stars, embroidered the earth with vegetation and animals, and then – the best part of all – how he fashioned man out of the dust of the ground, breathed into him his own spirit and made him like God himself. All in the space of six days, for on the seventh day God rested!

How accessible God is as a character in his own story, in the story of our beginning. Not a distant deity but one like ourselves: approachable, artistic, creative, thoughtful, full of kindness, in love with all he has made. As he surveys his handiwork at the end of each day, he says to himself: 'It is good'. But when it is completed with the appearance of mankind his final verdict is one of unconcealed pleasure: 'It is *very* good'.

Even when Adam sins the Almighty treats him gently. The full blame is shifted onto the snake in Paradise and a Saviour is promised who will crush the serpent's head, destroying its power for ever. The weakness of man before temptation simply demonstrates what we were already told, that he is partly dust.

As well as inheriting God's breath which gives him dignity, he is born out of the ground which leaves him vulnerable to shame. And yet his Creator loves him for all his earthiness. So his story does not end. It goes on to an epic future beyond Eden, a long running serial that is still being told but whose final episode will be the most exciting and splendid of all.

This fable from Genesis took more than five centuries to reach its final form. It was told from generation to generation many times before it came right. The ancient forefathers of the Jewish race spun variations of the tale for their children around their campfires in the desert night. Beneath the spangled constellations they unfurled the ancient myth to their spellbound audience.

They were not concerned that one day science would describe the beginning of things in different terms: as a big bang in the universe, as evolution, as natural selection. Nor does this bother us who re-read these biblical texts today.

Those venerable storytellers felt instinctively, as the Church still does, that the golden grains of truth contained in their stories were so true, they could have had no other author but God himself.

They were right. The Creation story is not concerned with *how* the world began but *why* – a much more important question! It also assures us that God's goodness is so great he can turn the tragedy of sin into victory. It consoles us in our own experience of evil and counsels us not to despair. It places the beauty of the world we inhabit in the context of a stage setting, a backdrop against which the drama of salvation is played out. It encourages us to go forward, like Adam and his wife, to find our redemption through work and family relationships and even through death.

Small wonder that this venerable book, though ancient, still satisfies the modern mind. For people don't change as people. Whichever age we belong to, few can resist a good read – especially when the narrative carries also in its pages the promise of grace and of life.

2

Facing the Truth

The Bible is essentially a book of stories in which God reveals himself through the thousands of tales which were gathered and cherished by the Jews of old and handed down to us as Sacred Scripture. Those stories are important not only because of what they reveal about God, but also because of what they reveal about us.

Human beings are very complex creatures. Our emotions run deep. The reasons that ground our actions are often hard to identify. Much of what motivates us remains hidden. We do not always understand the way we work. And sometimes this makes it difficult for us to face up to ourselves.

We refuse to acknowledge when we have done wrong because we are confused by our feelings. Anger or hurt or fear distort our vision of the truth of what we have done to others and cause us to justify our unkindness or bitterness or revenge. What we would immediately perceive as wrong if someone else did it becomes excusable in ourselves.

We are not alone in such self-deception. Scripture is full of sinners who were adept at evading their guilt. One way that God brought them to their senses and helped them face the facts was through the medium of story.

The classic example of this was King David. Basically a good individual and an excellent king, he was nevertheless a weak man at times who tried to deny his weakness by ignoring it. On one occasion he did serious harm to another man's marriage and, indeed, to his life.

Uriah the Hittite was the most loyal soldier in David's

army. While the king lounged idly at home Uriah was on the battlefield risking everything he had for Israel. During one such war David took advantage of Uriah's absence and sent for and seduced the soldier's wife, Bathsheba, who conceived a child. To make matters worse, David had Uriah placed in the thick of the fighting and ordered the troops to be withdrawn. When the assault was at its height Uriah was mown down by Israel's enemies. Then the King took Bathsheba to his own house and made her his wife.

Adultery and murder are not pretty words for describing one's actions, so David put such terms out of his mind and got on with the business of living. But sin is sin and God could not ignore the injustice. He sent his prophet Nathan to the King to make him acknowledge his fault.

How does one tell a king that he has committed a grievous wrong? Nathan did it by composing a story. 'There was once a poor man', said the prophet, 'who owned a little ewe lamb that was as dear to him as his child. It fed at his table and slept at his breast and was like a daughter to him'. The King listened with interest and, no doubt, some amusement. Here was a good diversion from his own troubles, an entertaining fable.

'In that same town lived a rich man,' continued the prophet, 'who owned many flocks and herds. One day a traveller arrived as his guest. It was no beast however from his own fields that the rich man slaughtered to feed him, but the little ewe lamb.' David's anger flared. 'Who is that man?' he cried. 'He deserves to die for this deed!' And Nathan replied, 'You are the man'.

David was forced to face the truth. Not through God's anger. Not through any stormy recriminations of the prophet. But through the simple clarity of a story well-told. David hung his head in profound shame. 'I have sinned against the Lord,' he confessed. It was the first step in his journey back to grace, the moment of repentance, the beginning of personal maturity.

How can a story achieve all this? And so diplomatically

too? It is because stories make you objective. We only fail to admit we are wrong if we are too closed in on ourselves to see what is what. By projecting our actions on to other characters we see them for what they really are. From a distance we can judge them critically.

A sin is wrong no matter who commits it. Injustice is evil even if I am responsible for it. Even if I have so dulled my conscience on the matter so that it no longer functions as it should. This will happen for instance if we continually repeat the same fault: eventually we become so used to it that it loses its gravity for us, we grow immune to its seriousness. If we could find a way to look objectively at it again, in another context, another light, our conscience would recover its former health and so save us from the sickness that leads to spiritual death.

This is what happens when we make a good confession. We tell the story of our sinfulness. We compose it for God, making ourselves the main character, confessing the action to be our responsibility. We make it a true story because God only listens to truth. And because we believe that he can transform our story by entering into it himself, making it turn out right. He does so when, like David, we see it from his perspective. When we stop changing the details to suit our pride or to excuse ourselves from what is inexcusable.

Once the story is told – objectively and honestly – then it ceases to be the nightmare that holds us down. It has no more control over us. Instead we gain control over it and over all it represents – our behaviour and our actions, our decisions and motives. All these we place under the inspiration of the Divine Storyteller, allowing him to rewrite the failures of the past in terms of his mercy and compose the next chapter of our life in terms of his grace. When the book of our life is complete and we look back at all the tales it tells, such stories as this will be among those we cherish most. They will be told in eternity to our credit and to God's glory.

3

Visions and Dreams

ven a quick glance through the Bible will uncover an amazing fact about the stories it contains: so many of them are accounts of dreams! Has it ever struck you as odd that a book which is supposed to be about reality should give such prominence to the fiction of the sleeping mind?

The dream of Abraham as he gazed upon the stars in the night sky is the starting-point of Bible history proper, the beginning of the Hebrew people. Much is made of his son Jacob's dream in which the famous ladder appeared, spanning the space between heaven and earth, with angels ascending and descending. How mysterious! His son, Joseph (of the coat of many colours), was known as the Dreamer because he fantasized so much! In fact his brothers hated to hear about his fantasies because in them they were always made out to be less distinguished than he.

Ezekiel had visions of the glorious Temple in Jerusalem even when it was reduced to dust and ashes. Daniel was the interpreter par excellence of Nebuchadnezar's terrifying nightmares. The New Testament opens with no less than five dreams: four of them attributed to St Joseph, husband of Mary. St Paul planned his missionary journeys according to his night-time inspirations, and the Bible closes with the Apocalypse ('A Dream Vision' in Greek), in which the writer describes the epic apparition of the New Jerusalem, the Kingdom of Heaven.

Obviously there is a lot more to dreams than we had thought. Otherwise, why were they reverently preserved as part of the inspired word of God? Maybe the answer lies in that word 'inspired'. Dreams inspire us. Behind every great man there is a great inspiration. Behind every advance in progress is a dream of better things to come.

Dreams are essential to a better future. They unleash the human imagination which leaps over everything that mere mortals call impossible. Think of man's landing on the moon. What an impossible dream that was even a hundred years ago. Yet someone envisioned it before it came true. Indeed someone's dream made it come true. Without the imagination we would still be hibernating in caves or swinging from trees.

God is the greatest dreamer of all. He created the human imagination. From his vision of things as they might be proceed all our most fantastic hopes and ambitions. Remember what the angel said to Mary in her vision: 'Nothing is impossible to God'! So when Abraham dreamed that he could have as many offspring as there were stars in the sky, that was God dreaming of his future Chosen People. The mysterious ladder of Jacob's dream, that was God planning a time when the chasm between him and us caused by our sin would be bridged by Christ.

When St Joseph dreamt of what he must do at the Nativity of Jesus, that was God bringing his dream of salvation safely to birth. And in the Apocalypse, when heaven was thrown open to the eyes of the mystic who saw it, that was nothing less than our heavenly Father dreaming of our coming home to him at the end of time.

Dreams are the stuff of which hope is made. Hope is what the Bible is about. On dark days when there is nothing to sustain us, God's hope keeps us going. The promise of a better day tomorrow. God does not break his promises. When the darkness becomes terrible, the memory of those promises provides a light. Our dreams refresh the memory of his trustworthiness. They stay with us till the moment we awake to the reality of their fulfilment.

This is why we go back again and again to the word of God. Just as at the Transfiguration Jesus gave his disciples a foretaste of his glory before Good Friday, so in the Scriptures the Holy Spirit inspires us with an assurance of victory over every dark night. To sit with the gospel open before us and read quietly with imagination alert is to have our personal nightmares put back into perspective. No matter what problems assail us, whatever mistakes we have made in the past, no matter what dread lies ahead, the image of Jesus, his death and resurrection, is a vision that encourages.

Just to ponder his hopes and dreams for us on the cross, simply to consider the lengths he went to in order to make his dream come true, is to see the meaning of all darkness. His passion interprets our pain positively, his ascension in glory indicates where it is leading us. Once the dream we are living here and now is reviewed in this way it begins to make sense. Suddenly everything that happens has a purpose. It is part of God's purpose, woven – like all the odd and confusing fragments that make up life – into the great design of his divine understanding.

Learn to cherish your dreams! They are the prayers of your imagination. Raise them to Christ so that through them he might reveal to you the deepest aspirations of your heart. Then simply believe that God never inspires hopes that he himself cannot fulfil.

4

The Flower in the Bud

People sometimes ask why we bother to read the Old Testament since we are Christians and the Old Testament is really Jewish literature. Surely now that Christ has come we no longer need the tales of what went before. His teaching is enough for us, his life ample for our salvation. Yet on most days of the year the first reading at Mass is from the prophets or the sagas of Israel's history.

Obviously the Church does not think the Old Testament irrelevant, and she is right. It has been her tradition right from the start to keep the pages of Jewish scripture open even as she proclaims the New Testament. This is because our religion is Judaeo-Christian, that is to say it has its roots in God's revelation to the Hebrew nation.

Christ's coming is a blossoming of the promises made from of old. Therefore we cannot fully appreciate what Jesus means to us until we look back into the hopes and expectations of our fathers. What God gave them in the bud, as it were, he has given to us in the flower. Flower and bud, together they make up one reality: salvation.

That is why it would be a great mistake to close up the book of the Old Testament, to cut the Bible in half and read only what suited us. If you prune the bud off the branch, how can you expect the blossom that produces the fruit? We cherish the characters of revelation before Christ and the stories of their lives, since they prefigure Jesus, shed light on the meaning of his life and death and his victory over sin. Let's take a couple of examples that illustrate what I mean.

Samson, in the Book of Judges, was a man of mighty strength, the scourge of his enemies, the Philistines, who could never get the better of him. This was because his strength lay in his closeness to God to whom his life was dedicated. He was a Nazirite from birth and the mark of his commitment to the Lord was his unshorn hair. While his hair remained uncut he was invincible.

Samson's only weakness lay in his love for a woman who was unworthy of him. Deceitful Delilah betrayed him to the Philistines by shearing the locks of his head when he lay asleep on her lap. She had egged him on to tell her the secret of his might – a thing he was not permitted to do – and for love's sake he told her, leaving himself vulnerable before her.

But as Samson stood chained between the two pillars of the mansion where the Philistines made sport of him, his hair began to grow again. Unknown to them, his strength returned. So he leaned his weight on the pillars, encircled them with his brawny arms, and pulled them down so that the mansion collapsed. Samson died in the rubble but so did three thousand Philistines with him. Thus, says the scripture, he killed more of his enemies at his death than he ever did in his life.

There is a wisdom in this story which matches our experience of life. Love does make fools of us. It makes us vulnerable and weak, and we do not care. When love is betrayed it can even destroy us. And yet by counting love greater than life the lover wins both in the end and emerges victorious.

Test the truth of this wisdom against the story of Jesus and see what it produces. As God's Son he was all-powerful and invincible, like Samson. But his love for a treacherous woman – the Church – made him set aside his glory and take on the weakness of mortal flesh. Revealing the source of his power over evil – his divine oneness with God his Father – he exposed himself to the jealous hatred of the Pharisees who had him crucified.

Like Samson his arms were pinned (to the cross) while his enemies, passing by, ridiculed and mocked him. Unknown to them, however, this weakness was Jesus' strength for by his suffering he was perfectly fulfilling his Father's will. At Calvary therefore Jesus brought down with him, not merely the mansion of the Philistines but the House of Satan, destroying the entire host of the forces of evil. Thus did he rout more of his enemies at his death than he ever exorcised in his life in Galilee.

Let's take another example, this time Daniel. Because this pious Hebrew, an exile in Babylon, refused to compromise with evil by giving up his daily prayer to God, he was condemned to be thrown into a den of famished lions. King Darius was distraught, for Daniel was his friend. Yet the law could not be altered even by the King and so, when the sun went down, the courageous young man was cast into the ravenous pit, 'and a stone was brought and laid upon the mouth of the den' to seal it (Dan 6:17).

Night passed. Then at break of day the King hurried to the mouth of the pit and called, 'O Daniel, servant of the living God, has your God, whom you serve continually, been able to deliver you from the lions?' (6:19-20). The young man's voice arose from the depths. 'O King, my God sent his angel and shut the lions' mouths and they have not hurt me, because I was found blameless before him' (6:22). So Daniel was taken up out of the den while those who condemned him took his place and were promptly devoured by the jaws of the beasts.

If the Samson story makes us think of Jesus' passion, the tale of Daniel cannot but recall Christ's burial and resurrection. Both men are figures or types of Jesus, in their fidelity to God, in their endurance of torture and betrayal, and in the justification of their lives by the manner of their deaths. If these stories move us, how much more ought we be moved when re-reading the accounts of Jesus in the light of lesser heroes.

But more than that – these are all *sacred stories*, and as

such they engage Truth. Not in the sense of being factually true, for they are stories and not history. But in that they form part of what has been handed down to us as divine revelation. They reveal a truth that Jesus fulfils, which he brings to completion. They unfold the way God works, who is truth, and who by showing us his truth saves the world. These stories have power to do what no other stories can. Reflected upon, they put us in direct touch with the mind of God and bring us a grace that can change us. Can you think of any better reason for reading the Old Testament?

5

The Traveller's Tale

No great literature is without its travel stories. They form a particular genre or type of writing which is as ancient, and as modern, as story-telling itself. We think of some of the most famous in the English language: Robert Louis Stevenson's *Travels With A Donkey*, Tim Severin's *The Brendan Voyage*, or the journals of H.V. Morton which were so popular up to some years ago. The forerunner of these was Chaucer's *Canterbury Tales*, the fourteenth century saga of pilgrims on their way to the shrine of St Thomas à Becket, and the unforgettable yarns they spun to pass the time and shorten the tedious route.

Not too surprising then to find that the travel story is very much part of biblical literature. The inspired Jewish and Christian writers of the Old and New Testaments obviously sensed a tremendous spiritual significance in the theme of travelling since they used it so much to record their experiences of God. St Luke, for example, presents the story of Jesus in terms of his fateful journey to Jerusalem, to his cross and resurrection. And in the Acts of the Apostles the remarkable spread of the early Church from Palestine to Rome is retold as the adventure of Paul on his missionary voyages.

But the journey of God's people really begins in the Old Testament epic of the Exodus, itself the most thrilling travel story ever written. Like most other classical epics, such as Homer's *Odyssey* or the Celtic Wandering Aengus, it was passed down by word of mouth for many generations before being committed to paper. The final author's genius was in selecting the best of the oral traditions and putting them together in a meaningful way that gave them enduring significance.

Like these others too, the Exodus has its epic hero – Moses. He did what no other man would dare: he challenged the Egyptian Pharaoh to release his Hebrew people from slavery to seek the Promised Land of their dreams. After many trials he succeeded. First, he led the tribes of Israel through the Red Sea in which Pharaoh's forces were drowned, and then brought them through the Sinai desert where they wandered for forty years till they reached the country of their destiny.

What makes the story biblical is the fact that God was the real force behind their journey to freedom. It was he who called Moses to act on his behalf, to pronounce the Law that cemented the covenant and unite the homeless nomads into a single religious community. At every turn on the way they sensed his hidden presence.

He seemed to anticipate their every need. When they were hungry in the barren wilderness with nothing to eat, he provided manna from heaven for them. But could he quench their thirst in this arid desert? Yes he could. They discovered springs of water gushing from the rock. Amazing, they cried. Each miraculous piece of good fortune helped them to survive the harshest experiences of their forty years wandering. Eventually they would look back at this time as one of the best in their relationship with Yahweh. Never had he been so close to them, or they to him.

What sets the Exodus apart from other travel tales is its sacramental relevance. It bespeaks the life-journey of God's people in every age.

How often we think of this present existence as a desert. When we run out of resources to deal with problems we talk of spiritual dryness, or weariness of soul, or emotional hunger. When we meet disappointment, when friends let us down, we see happiness vanish like a mirage in the heat. If we repeat our mistakes we think of ourselves as slaves under bondage. Subconsciously we are using the language and imagery of the Exodus. We identify with the fate of the Hebrews under Moses.

At such moments God is as close to us as he was to them. Through the sacramental life of the Church he re-plays his great deeds of the past all over again in us. By his forgiveness in confession, for example, he sets us free from the tyranny of sin just as he liberated the Israelites from Egypt. As he once led them safely through the waters of the Red Sea so he delivers us through the waters of baptism, not from Pharaoh, but from Satan's power. When we require nourishment for the long trek ahead, he feeds us with the Eucharist – the true manna from heaven. And in our spiritual thirst which no water can satisfy, he gives us his Spirit, a well-spring of refreshment that bubbles up from within our hearts, stony though they sometimes be. To all this he adds the hope of a Promised Land at journey's end. Not Canaan, as in the Moses story, but heaven itself.

The truth of the Exodus becomes reality for us in our life in the Church or, more properly speaking, our life *as* the Church. Through the sacraments we are called to a voyage out of ourselves, our sinfulness, our isolation. This odyssey is a search for our true selves and it happens through the phases of our development as human beings towards maturity.

We are not allowed to settle down in our childhood, we must pass on into adolescence. From young adulthood we must break camp again and move to the regions of middle age and elderliness. No matter how we might wish to go back, to return to a former time of youth and health like the Hebrews in the desert who wanted to go back to the security of Egypt, we cannot.

But at each stage of the journey there is a sacrament to guide us into the right choices and decisions that mark the route to freedom. Baptism is for the beginning of the itinerary, Confirmation for the adolescent, Matrimony or Holy Orders for young adulthood, the Anointing of the

Sick for old age. And for everyone, daily if necessary, Eucharist and Reconciliation to see us through the rough parts of the path. With these helps we track grace in new ways, observe new aspects of God's goodness, his understanding, his moral support. And so we grow as God intended.

Nor are we alone. Many fellow travellers accompany us, sharing the same desert, struggling towards the same maturity that we seek. Leading us we have our own Moses – Jesus himself. In him we find God. By keeping in his track we have God's word on oath that we shall also find ourselves.

6

Of Ghouls and Ghosts

as it Robbie Burns who penned the prayer:
'From ghoulies and ghosties and long-legged
beasties, and things that go bump in the night,
Good Lord deliver us'? Well, like the Scots poet country
people still love to gather round the hearth on dark nights,
switch off the TV and exchange tales of the macabre. Such
tales usually make us sit close to one another, prevent
arguments, and cause us to go home in pairs or threes!
Wonderful community-binders!

The word of God has its ghost story too – one that
would chill your spine if you read it alone at night! I
wonder why the Bible preserved it for us? We'll come to
that in a moment.

Saul was King of Israel when David was still a young
man. But towards the end of his life he fell away from God
and failed to pray as he ought. His last battle with the
Philistines was weighing on his mind. He worried and
fretted about its outcome until it became an obsession. No
answer came to him from God, so Saul decided to do
something that was very dangerous and strictly forbidden.
He would consult the witch of Endor.

He himself had banished all witches and mediums from
the land during his wiser days. So he went to her in disguise
in case she refused to help him. 'Call up a spirit from the
grave,' he ordered, 'that I may know if I should do battle
with the Philistine'. 'Whom do you wish me to summon?'
she inquired, and he told her, 'Samuel the prophet'.

A shape appeared through the smoke: an old man
wrapped in a robe, emerging from the depths of the earth.

The woman screamed when she saw him. 'You have deceived me,' she cried to the king, 'You are Saul!' But Saul was crazed to know what no man ought to know. 'Tell me,' he shouted, 'what shall I do? God has turned away and answers me no more!'

And Samuel's reply made the king turn so faint with distress that he fell to the ground in a faint. 'God has not turned away from you,' said the prophet. 'You have turned from God. The Lord will give you into the hands of your enemies, and tomorrow you and your sons will be with me among the dead.' His words came true. One account of the story suggests that Saul was mortally wounded next day on the battle field and that, rather than be slain by the Philistine, he took his own life by falling upon his sword.

So why was this story so important to the Jews that it became part of their Bible? Because it expresses clearly God's anger with those who deal in the occult and demonstrates how serious the consequences of such practice can be. Psychological distress, despair, even suicide – as in Saul's case – are fearful possibilities when people meddle with the powers of darkness.

The very first commandment – 'No other gods but me' – includes within its meaning a ban on black magic. Saul lost his peace with God when he defied that injunction. Turning to witchcraft was itself a sign that he had abandoned the Lord.

Temptation to follow the occult – superstition, astrology, ouija boards, whatever – isn't it a symptom of having given up the true practice of religion? Man is religious by nature. When he falls away from worship and prayer his natural religious instinct will still seek an outlet. If a person cuts himself off from faith in God, what other outlet is there for him to find?

It is interesting today to note how the rise in non-practising young people is accompanied by a rise in the incidence of pagan rites or festivals. Stonehenge at the mid-summer solstice, for example; the New Age movement;

the reports of Satanism in the newspapers from time to time.

Superstition is contrary to the teaching of Jesus as it was to that of Moses. St Paul tells us that Christ, by his Resurrection and Ascension to the Father's right hand, has put under his foot every authority and dominion in this age and the age to come. He has subjected the elemental spirits of the universe and disarmed all principalities and powers (Eph 1:21-22; Col 2:8,15). The same St Paul did more than preach this message. He acted on it by rooting out all the books of magic he could find when he arrived in Ephesus on his second missionary journey. The Acts of the Apostles recounts the event in stirring narrative style.

While Paul was in the city he dispossessed some Ephesians of evil spirits in the name of Jesus. Impressed by the results, the seven sons of a Jewish high priest tried to do the same. The consequences were terrifying. The man with the evil spirit leaped on them, mastered all of them, and overpowered them, so that they fled out of that house naked and wounded.

When the story got round, all the residents of Ephesus, Jews and Greeks alike, were seized with fear. Many turned to faith in Christ, confessed their sinister practices, and brought their books of magic art to be burned in public. We are told that when the value of the literature destroyed was counted up, it came to fifty thousand pieces of silver! (Acts 19:11-19). You can imagine how widespread black magic had become before the arrival of Christianity.

The benefit of tales like these from the Old and New Testament is easy to see. The message they convey comes across so much more vividly through the story-form than, say, in the form of a commandment such as 'Thou shalt not dabble in witchcraft'. The consequences of getting involved with the occult are immediately apparent. The displeasure of God becomes understandable.

But best of all, the solution to the problem also shines out clearly. When we turn to Jesus and acknowledge him as Lord of the universe, we have a power that is greater than any other. In him the forces of evil are vanquished, and those who have experienced the snare of Satan are set free.

Maybe it's time that young people in our inner city areas should be encouraged to read the story of King Saul and St Paul, and be helped to interpret what God is saying to us all through these narratives.

7

The Jungle Book

The best literature is about people. That's what keeps us reading fiction, fairytale and folklore. Personalities, and what they get up to. The effect that men and women have on each other's lives. A very complex subject of course, given the subtle way people think and act. We may say one thing and mean another. The motive we profess for doing something may well be far from the truth. We can some times feel two opposite emotions at the same time and behave in a most confusing manner!

One way that good writers explore the quirks in human nature is to project these on to animal characters in the form of a fable. One thinks of Aesop's amusing story of the fox and the crow which illustrated the victory of cunning over pride.

Then there was Kenneth Graham's charming *Wind In The Willows* where every human type appeared in the creatures of the river-bank: the naive little Mole, dependable Ratty, wise Badger, vicious Stoat and – best of all – the all too-human Toad with his silly pride and self-importance and yet his desire to be normal and liked.

In the 1940's George Orwell's classic tale, *Animal Farm*, was banned in the Soviet Union because his portrayal of Communism as a revolt of swine was so obvious an attack on their political system.

The biblical writers were first in this tradition: they led the way. Not by animating the animals as in a Walt Disney cartoon, but by using them as symbols of human realities. Take the serpent in Paradise for example. Satan in viper's disguise. What a wonderful image for examining the diabolical mind of evil! When we are tempted to do wrong it is because we suppose it is good. That's the way temptation works. How appropriate to think of a serpent. In Disney's 'Jungle Book' the snake is dangerous, deceitful, hypnotic, spell-binding, just as in the Book of Genesis. We sympathize as God himself did with poor Eve who was enthralled out of her reason by the serpent.

We sympathize also with ourselves, so often ensnared by the same trick. And we laugh too – a wonderful way to react when we laugh with the truth of God's insight.

In the New Testament Jesus called Herod 'that old fox'! Not like Jesus as we usually think of him, but he was right. Herod was cunning, to be watched carefully, especially when you spoke to him. So Jesus remained silent in his presence.

But the Bible also used animals to explore the nature of God. When the prophet Isaiah thought about the world as it would one day be under God's reign, he described it as a mountain menagerie. There the wolf would dwell with the lamb, the leopard would lie down with the goat-kid, the calf and lion and the fatling would rest together. The cow and the bear would feed side by side, the lion would eat straw like the ox, and little children would play safely around the adder's den, even putting their hands down into its burrow.

What Isaiah envisaged was a world at peace. A place where all the aggressive human instincts symbolized by the lion and bear and leopard and adder, would be reconciled with man's better nature – the lamb, the kid, the calf, the child. No words could have conveyed his meaning better. How his listeners must have rejoiced to hear of such a universe redeemed by God.

We can go even further with our biblical animals. The three Persons of the Holy Trinity are likened to birds of the air. In the Old Testament, God the Father is compared with the eagle. 'You have seen,' Yahweh reminds his people, 'how I bore you on eagles' wings and brought you to myself', recalling their deliverance from Egypt (Ex19:4). In the Book of Deuteronomy the image is repeated. There Moses sings of God's goodness to Israel. 'Like an eagle that stirs up its nest, that flutters over its young, spreading out its wings, catching them, bearing them on its pinions, the Lord alone did lead Israel' (32:11). It is the very picture of God's strength and fidelity, qualities in him that do not change.

Similarly in the New Testament when we come to God's Son. Jesus stands weeping upon the Mount of Olives overlooking Jerusalem just before his passion and death. It is the start of Holy Week, the last days of his life. Here is a city that will soon be in ruins despite all his attempts to help it.

In half a century his vision would come true; the Romans would attack Jerusalem, leaving not a stone upon a stone. In his grief for what might have been, Jesus sobs, 'O Jerusalem, Jerusalem! How often would I have gathered your children together as a hen gathers her brood under her wings, and you would not!' (Mt 23:37). It is a vivid and emotional representation of Jesus' character: protective, compassionate, forgetful of self, very maternal. Like a mother hen distracted for her chicks. Such was Christ's extraordinary love for sinners.

And finally, the Holy Spirit. He appears in the pages of revelation in the guise of a dove. Overshadowing Jesus at his baptism in the Jordan, he is the symbol of peace, a new world-order, anointing Christ for his work of redemption.

One is reminded of the dove over the ark in the Noah story, announcing the end of the deluge and the emergence of the new creation washed clean of sin after the flood. The Spirit of God was metaphorically on the wing in that fable, for where the Spirit is there follows concord and order.

It was the same at the very beginning, in the first few verses of the Bible at the first creation. Out of the chaos of the void through the darkness that lay on the face of the

31

deep, suddenly there appeared 'the Spirit of God moving over the face of the waters' (Gen 1:2). His flight brought immediate change: light and life and goodness. He still achieves these changes in us when we permit him to sweep across the dark depths of our soul.

The value of the Bible's animal images becomes apparent only when we meditate upon them. At first they may surprise us, even appear irreverent. But keep this in mind: they are given to us as revelation. They represent the way God wishes us to think about himself and his great kindness towards human beings.

8

Seeking God's Guidance

mong the difficult decisions Jesus had to make during his ministry was whom should he choose to be his Apostles? These were to be his close friends who would bear witness to his death, proclaim his resurrection, and set the world on fire with faith after his ascension. Before short-listing the finalists, St Luke tells us, Jesus spent the night in prayer. He was Son of Man as well as Son of God. He needed God's guidance in such an important move.

The next morning he made his selection. And what a disaster they turned out to be! Judas betrayed him into the hands of his enemies. Peter denied him outright after the arrest. All of them fled when he needed them most on the cross. Thomas refused to believe he had risen from the dead – he wanted scientific proof! Two of them, James and John, hankered after rank in the kingdom. Nathaniel, the cynic, did not believe there would be a kingdom at all. Matthew was a plain, old-fashioned swindler. And Simon the Zealot was an ex-terrorist. What a crew to build a Church on!

Did Jesus then make a dreadful mistake? Not in the least. God's plan came to its perfect fulfilment through each one of them. That is why we have the Apostolic Church today, the Creed, the gospels, the sacraments, and the hope of eternal life.

What Luke's story makes clear – and he repeats the lesson throughout the Gospel – is that when you pray as Christ did, you will receive wisdom to make the correct move. Having brought the matter to God, do what you feel is right and leave the rest to him. Learning to be at peace about this is what we call discernment.

Even if things should go wrong afterwards, there need be no self recriminations. God himself knows that we can only do what we see fit at the time. He knows too that our vision is limited.

We cannot foresee the consequences of present choices. When we admit this and ask God – whose knowledge includes the future – to direct us, then he bears responsibility for the way things turn out as much as we do. If a mistake is made, then it is his. Since God does not make mistakes, we ought not to worry.

Those same Apostles took a leaf out of Jesus' book when they began to spread his message and his Church. According to the Acts of the Apostles (also written by St Luke) they prayed together every time a crisis arose or an important new step had to be taken. In choosing a replacement for Judas, for example, they asked God to show them whom to select. Later, when the opposition against them increased they gathered again to ask how to speak out. Before appointing the seven deacons they sought divine approval.

As Paul and his companions set out on their first missionary journey from Antioch the whole community invoked God's guidance with prayer and fasting. And when the question arose about admitting the Gentiles to the faith – a very thorny problem for Christians of Jewish background – the issue was settled by the discernment of the Council at Jerusalem. And so it goes on. Story after story, example after example.

It is no coincidence that the author of these stories is the same man. Luke believed, as all his writings show, that the Holy Spirit is the life and soul of the Church, its very breath and inspiration.

When men and women really wish to discern God's will in their lives, the Paraclete does not abandon them. Luke never actually says this in so many words but he shows it to be true in the way he composes his tales. Just as a picture is worth a thousand words, so a story contains more than a thousand explanations. The evangelist was fully aware of this.

At the start of his gospel, addressed to his friend Theophilus, he confessed that he had taken a great deal of trouble to get these stories right. They were obviously very important to him. 'Inasmuch as many have undertaken to compile a narrative (about Jesus and his Spirit), just as they were delivered to us...by eyewitnesses and ministers of the word, it seemed good to me also, having followed all things closely for some time past, to write an orderly account for you...that you may know the truth'(Lk 1:1-4).

What made him such a good story-teller was not just that he researched his facts thoroughly, but that he arranged them in such a way as to communicate the heart of the matter. He was not writing a history of Jesus or a biography. His aim was to present the meaning of Christ's coming and to announce the power he left behind when he sent his Spirit from the Father

Nor did he see these events as something in the past. He wanted to show how that same power of Christ's life, death and resurrection is with us till the end of time. Because of our faith we can all live as God wants us to live, close to the truth and guided by truth in every circumstance that challenges us.

To demonstrate how this is done he begins the gospel narrative with the story of the Annunciation to the Virgin Mary. It is the classic tale of Christian discernment. Mary is confused and afraid at the approach of the heavenly messenger. How can she be sure this is not a demon disguised as an angel of light? She listens as Gabriel speaks God's word. Then she questions him. 'What does this mean? How can this be?' She recognizes the truth in his reply, 'Nothing is impossible to God.'

What he tells her fits in with her knowledge of Old Testament scripture; then she learns about Elizabeth's pregnancy – her ancient relative has conceived! Finally, having thought it through intelligently as far as her reason allowed, she makes her act of faith. 'Behold the handmaid of the Lord. Let it be done according to your word.'

Mary's was already a prayerful spirit, a meditative heart. She was ready for the guidance of the Holy Spirit when he came to her. She recognized him in her own story as the angel narrated it. Before she conceived the Word in her womb, she nourished that Word in her mind and heart. In her story, as in the stories of Jesus and the Apostles, St Luke is showing us that we can make difficult decisions with confidence too. We do so when we allow God's Wisdom and Love into the decision-making process and then entrust the outcome to his dependable providence.

9

A Winter's Tale

The Nativity story's winter setting is part of the magic that enchants us at Christmas: the cold of the shelter where the baby was laid, the warmth of the animals' breath, the deep snow all around, the frost brought in by the shepherds as they kneel to adore at the manger. And on our Christmas cards, the December robin perched on the berried holly which flourishes in the winter season.

But the gospel accounts of Jesus' birth make no mention of winter. In fact they give no clue in which month the Christ-child was born. Yet the Church chooses dark December as the ideal time to celebrate the story of God's coming into our midst as an infant exposed to the chill of the world's indifference. So how, we may ask, did the Nativity of Our Lord Jesus Christ come to be a Winter's tale?

It began in the fourth century when the Nativity was first celebrated in the churches Rome. Before then, only the Easter festival interrupted the daily round of the liturgical calendar. Then came the first Christian Emperor, Constantine, and suddenly all Rome was baptised.

As pagans these people had been accustomed to keeping the mid-winter feast of *Saturnalia*, a traditional time of revelry and fun. At the winter solstice, the moment when the sun reaches its most distant point from the northern hemisphere, pauses, and seems to return again, they celebrated *Sol Invictus* – the Unconquered Sun!

All creation, which seemed to die at his absence, could now put off its weeds of mourning. The great Light had overcome the dread darkness of winter and by December 25th was already coming back to renew the earth in its new-born rays.

What a perfect foundation for a yearly Christian feast to honour the Unconquered Son of God! His appearance at Bethlehem was as timely as the return of spring. For the earth had been shrouded in the winter of sin and longed for the new life that God alone could bring. This Son of God would cause revelry and gladness by his ultimate victory over death itself. Christmas would lead spiritually and naturally to the April celebration of the Resurrection.

Thus the course of the Church's worship would match the cycle of the seasons from the start of each new year and help trace the growth in the light from death to life.

To see the Christmas story in the light of the natural world is to read it with greater understanding. If we look at nature carefully what we find is that it tells the gospel narrative in its own distinctive way. It's only natural that it should: God is the origin of both.

He who now reveals himself through his Son first revealed himself through his creation. Jesus is the Word made flesh; it was through that Word the Father called all things into being, including times and seasons and the cycle of birth and death and regeneration. Jesus is the Word through whom all things were made, the same Word that became flesh in the womb of Mary. The wisdom which was brought forth in the manger at Bethlehem for shepherds and Magi to see is the very wisdom that is imprinted upon the beauty of the year.

What is this wisdom? It is the fact that after every night comes a morning. That after every winter there is a spring. That after every sowing comes a reaping. So dependable is the pattern that farmers can plan their work ahead. They know when to put the crops in and when they will be ready for harvesting.

It is a lesson that Jesus put into words and action for us by his birth and death. 'Unless a seed falls to the ground and dies,' he once said, 'it remains only a single grain. But if it dies it yields a rich crop'. He was talking about people of course, not farming. But as it is with the crops so it is with us. Only when we are prepared to die to our selfishness for the sake of others do we grow like the seeds to maturity.

It was to teach us the truth and the wisdom of this that Jesus died on the cross. And it was in order to die that he was born. 'If any one wishes to save his life,' he remarked on another occasion, 'he must lose it; and anyone who loses his life for my sake and the sake of the gospel, will find it'.

The creation understands what he meant and does it all the time. Day willingly dies to night and summer gracefully gives way to winter. The seed patiently yields up its life in the earth and Christ willingly gave up his Spirit on the cross. God and nature collaborating in a unity of purpose to teach us the way to eternal life.

The Christmas story says it all in the delightful simplicity of the Nativity in the Magi who brought the infant a gift of myrrh. Myrrh was a precious preparation for the corpse before burial. It was a faith-filled acknowledge-ment of what Jesus had come to do.

Wise men understood the meaning of his birth from the beginning. They also brought him gold. A royal metal fit for a king. Jesus deserved such honour for the love that moved him to become a slave by dying for sinners. Their third gift was frankincense. A burning fragrance to accompany sacrifice. They saw in his incarnation the perfect sacrifice that cancels forever the punishment our sins deserved.

Only the wise appreciate the gospel. For the rest it is foolishness. The story of Bethlehem calls us to leave our foolishness aside and become wise men. The world of nature encourages us to do the same. By choosing mid-winter to re-tell the tale, the Church weds together the natural and the supernatural to remind us that God's truth is the same wherever you look for it. And to remind us of course that his love turns every Winter's Tale into a Mid-Summer Night's Dream.

Emmanuel

The most beautiful name by which Jesus is known in the Scriptures is Emmanuel, the name foretold by the prophet Isaiah more than seven centuries before Jesus was born.

St Matthew recalls the ancient prophecy in the opening pages of the New Testament and explains what it means. 'Behold, a virgin shall conceive and bear a son, and his name shall be called Emmanuel (which means, God with us).' It marks the beginning of his account of Christmas and ever since the rich and meaningful associations of that title have graced the hymns and prayers of the Church's celebration of the holy season.

To invoke Jesus as Emmanuel is the most profound act of Christian faith for it acknowledges that Mary's Son is at the same time Son of God. It is also a profound act of hope, for it announces the immense significance of the incarnation for a world that feels lost and alone and longs for a friend who will bring it understanding and direction.

When we think about that name Emmanuel we realise that God is with us in Jesus in more ways than one. Obviously he is with us as man in Jesus' humanity. By becoming a member of the human race Christ brings God very close to all of us. No longer remote and beyond our experience, he is one of our own kind. God knows what it is to live and breathe, to eat and sleep, to be happy and sad, to be unwell and to die. Because of Christmas we can relate to God in a human way confident that he understands our needs and problems and struggles. In Jesus he is a very human God. Quite literally with us in the flesh, in time and space, through the historical character of Mary's Son.

But there is another sense in which God is with us. In the sense that he gives strong moral backing to everything we do that is truly human. He takes our part in the battle of life against the odds which are weighted against us. He is on our side in the face of all that threatens to defeat us. Even when we fail to do our best, he is still 'rooting for us', giving the encouragement needed to help us get up and start again. Never putting us down by criticising our efforts or jeering at our mistakes, he actually affirms us by making excuses in our defence, and where no excuse is possible, by forgiving.

Jesus is truly God-with-us in this most important way. Which is why Christmas is such a joyful season. Pope St Leo the Great in a Christmas sermon once said that this joy is open to saint and sinner alike. For the saint because he hastens to his crown; but for the sinner because he is called to Life.

What makes all this good news is that it never ends. If God were Emmanuel only for the brief space of Jesus' life – the thirty three years lived two thousand years ago – then his name would be no use to us at all. But at the end of Matthew's Gospel Jesus announced, 'I am with you always, yes to the end of time'. I will always be Emmanuel, always God with you, he is saying. And so Matthew's Gospel ends as it begins, assuring us that God will never let us down since he is forever with us in both senses, both personally present and morally supportive.

How Jesus makes this possible is in and through the Church. He is as much among us now as he was when he walked the roads of Galilee and the streets of Jerusalem. Only the form of his presence is different.

Today he is with us in Word and Sacrament, where the scriptures are read and believed, and where the liturgy is celebrated worthily with a pure and contrite heart. Every time we listen to the readings at Mass, receive the Holy

Eucharist, go to confession, turn to him in prayer alone or with others, wherever 'two or three are gathered in his name', there Emmanuel fulfils the promise of his name.

To make this joy complete only one thing further is needed. This Christmas as we get into the festive mood we ought to be asking ourselves: Am I with God as much as God is with me?

11

A Night of Storytelling

The best stories beg to be dramatized. This is why good novels get turned into films, why we go to the theatre, and why we enjoy acting and role-play. It is no different where the gospel is concerned. The Church not only reads the story of Jesus aloud. She also enacts it in the ritual of the Mass and the sacraments – what we commonly call the liturgy. First the text, then its dramatization. Together, reading and ritual keep the message and meaning of Jesus before us through every day and season.

Once a year the Church sets aside a special night for such storytelling in word and action: the Easter Vigil of Holy Saturday which begins after sun-down. It is a sparkling festival of sound and light to mark the greatest feast of the Christian calendar, the Lord's resurrection from the dead.

The stories told during this night-watch shorten the hours of darkness for those who await the dawn. They breach the loneliness with the good fellowship that story-telling creates. They draw the community together in a spirit of growing excitement through the grand celebration of Jesus' victory over the tomb, which proclaims a new age of hope and exultation.

The festival begins with the 'Liturgy of Light', Act One of the drama of Easter. A great fire is made out under the stars of an April sky. As the flames leap up into the cold air, scattering sparks and devouring the darkness, the Paschal candle is solemnly raised on high. Five grains of incense representing the wounds on Christ's body are imprinted into the wax. The assembled crowd gathers round to see and to warm themselves with the glow of faith.

The Lordship of Jesus is proclaimed in clear tones in an otherwise silent scene. '*Alpha* and *Omega*, the Beginning and End.' All time belongs to him. The wind shifts the falling embers. A sense of peace and security ensconces the Church.

A taper touches the candle wick. '*Lumen Christi* – Light of Christ.' The new life is proclaimed. It is carried in procession into the darkened church. Baptismal candles are thrust into its flame. Soon the light spreads pew by pew as the whole congregation take their places. The building is aglow with shimmering lights – the spread of the Easter faith, like the spread of the gospel, illumines every dim corner, every eerie shadow.

A common voice is given to the Creed. Word and action: the beginnings of our faith in the Risen Lord have been mysteriously recalled and proclaimed in this opening theatrical scene of the greatest story ever told.

Act Two is the 'Liturgy of the Word'. Ritual needs to be articulated in human speech. The Word of God in the words of men. And so the nine readings of the night-vigil begin. They trace the story from the start. Salvation begins when God creates the world. Adam's sin does not interrupt God's saving love. As he created us, so he promises to redeem us.

The tale continues through the prophecies. A suffering Messiah will come to ease the suffering of sin and dispel the darkness of hell. Then St Paul and his proclamation of Jesus. Then the story from Matthew or Mark or Luke of the discovery of the empty tomb. The announcement of the angels: 'He is not here, he is risen as he promised! Go and tell!' The light which ignited our candles now ignites our hearts.

Next, the 'Liturgy of Water' as the story is repeated in symbol. The Easter Candle is plunged into the font as far as the flame and raised up out of it again. Three times. As

Jesus was plunged into the waters of the Jordan and immediately resurged, as he was plunged into the bowels of the grave and on the third day rose again, so the Easter water, blessed and sanctified by the drama of this holy night, will incorporate many new converts into his saving death and resurrection.

The action moves to the altar for the finale: the 'Liturgy of the Eucharist'. Here the bread and wine are made ready for the prayer of consecration. Like the water and fire before them, these are the elements of nature which God uses to communicate his saving grace. Drawn from the created world which has been redeemed by the incarnation, they are to make present not only the memory of the Paschal Mystery, but the Risen Lord himself. Jesus, personally present in sacrament as in word, becomes bread in our hands.

The host is raised above the heads of the congregation. The cup is lifted in blessing. Christ has joined us in the celebration as he promised he always would. For this theatrical replay of the event makes what it tells come true! The resurrection is not just a good tale from the past. It is an ever-present reality with power to change our lives.

Already the dawn streaks the eastern sky. Not outside in the still-darkened town or city. But inside the hearts of the faithful. The stone of the tomb of our soul has been rolled back and the light of Christ's love is already pouring in upon the emptiness of our daily lives. Filling that emptiness with meaning. Giving it new purpose as he calls us out of death with him to the fullness of life with God.

As the liturgy draws to a close with the ringing tones of the last Alleluia, the mood of the crowd filing out has changed. They came in at the start in whispers. Now they are talking freely and aloud. They entered the Church one by one or in small groups. Now they leave as one people. They arrived as Mary Magdalen arrived at the tomb – not sure quite what to expect. They leave as she left, having seen something that transforms our view of everything.

The way stories are told makes a difference. Good liturgy is the most effective means we have for encountering Christ. His story begs to be dramatized. And not only in Church but in the quality of our living. And not only at Easter but throughout the entire year.

12

God's Elderly Recruits

 am always amazed, when I read the Gospel accounts of Jesus' early years, to find how many elderly people fill the scenes. They positively crowd the stories of Jesus' infancy and dominate the events that mark his child hood.

To begin with we have Zachariah, the aged priest of the Jewish Temple, and Elizabeth his wife who is too old to bear children. They become the parents of John the Baptist. St Luke tells us that they are both advanced in years.

Then there is Joseph, the husband of Mary. Tradition suggests that he was not young. St Matthew's Gospel depicts him as a man of dreams, and medieval paintings of the Nativity often show him asleep with the tiredness of years.

When the infant Jesus is brought to Jerusalem to be presented in the Temple, another ancient figure comes forward to receive him. This is Simeon, an 'upright and devout man' who has spent his latter years religiously preparing for death. The Holy Spirit has promised him that he will not die until he beholds the Lord's Christ. His prayer, as he takes the holy Child in his arms, is one of joyful thanks for such a reward after a lifetime's waiting, one of serene acceptance of his end: 'Now, Master, you are letting your servant go in peace as you promised; for my eyes have seen the salvation which you have made ready in the sight of the nations'.

No sooner are these words uttered than in shuffles old Anna, a prophetess of great age. She is at least eighty-four, according to the Gospel. She gives an ecstatic cry of wonder and praise at Jesus' appearance. We are told that she spoke of him to all who were looking forward to the redemption of Jerusalem.

Isn't it odd that God should employ so many aged figures in this exceptionally important moment of history? In today's world a person finds it hard to get a job after forty, the retired are not even considered for positions of responsibility, and workers of long standing are often paid off or made redundant well before retirement age. God wouldn't stand a chance as an industrial manager in the new millennium!

Yet it seems he went out of his way to pick men and women in their autumn years to introduce the New Testament, to be Christ's first witnesses in the world, and to help the Virgin Mary in the earliest and most vulnerable days of her motherhood. The Gospel makes no secret of the fact that the young Mary depended totally on Joseph to guard her and her child from Herod, that she listened with reverential respect to the prophetic advice of Simeon and Anna, that she gladly accepted Zechariah's hospitality, and was deeply moved by the encouragement she received from Elizabeth.

Young people are no different today. Like Mary, they still need firm support from older people who believe in them if they are to do God's will and carry out his plans. The heavenly Father was wise to draft in recruits with experience and maturity of years to aid the mother of his Son. None is more eligible to affirm a young person than one who has spent a lifetime in prayer and has a regular pattern of spiritual practice. People like that are very much in touch with the mind of God and can sense instinctively what God wants the young to do.

I believe God still wants the elderly to help in this way today. We are mistaken if we think that modern teenagers know it all, that they don't need direction, or that they would resent being advised by anyone over fifty. Not so. In most cases young people are delighted when any one takes a genuine interest in their progress. How often do you hear

48

them complaining that parents misunderstand them, that they ignore them or don't appreciate their efforts.

Grandparents on the other hand are frequently on their Top Ten list. Why? Because Grandma and Grandpa are not frazzled like Mum and Dad are, and have more time to sit down and listen. They don't have to worry as parents do because they don't have the burden and responsibility of rearing them.

The older generation can afford to be relaxed with their grandchildren. They are freer to discuss issues of concern. Like Elizabeth, Simeon, Anna, Zechariah and Joseph in the Gospel, they mellow with wisdom and grace. They know goodness when they see it, and are not afraid to thank God aloud when they recognize it. No wonder the young respond to them so easily.

If you are elderly, perhaps you could leave aside your own problems for a while today, and just talk to some young ones about themselves. They'll probably sing a joyful *Magnificat* to God for you if you do, and remember you for a very long time to come. And you may even make a significant difference in their lives.

13

A Divine Sense of Humour

People occasionally remark how strange it is that we never see Jesus laughing in the Gospels. And it's true. God is shown actually laughing only twice in the entire Bible, in the Book of Psalms. Even there, it is the laughter of scorn for his enemies, not the merry, good natured laugh we so enjoy in life.

Does that mean that God has no sense of humour? I don't believe so. Some of the funniest comics on television are those who keep a straight face when telling a joke. As I see it, that's what God does in the Scriptures too.

Take the time the Lord promised Abraham that he would become the father of a multitude. The old man must have nearly died, for he was seventy-five years old. By the time he was ninety-nine, the child still hadn't appeared. No wonder he began to get worried! Had the Lord only been pretending? Not a bit of it. The baby wasn't due till Abraham turned a hundred.

Obviously no one had bothered to inform Sarah about this plan because when she learned that she was to become pregnant, she started to giggle. Suddenly Abraham saw the funny side of it too. 'Is a child to be born to a man one hundred years old,' he asked, 'and will Sarah have a child at the age of ninety?' And quite literally he fell to the ground on his face and roared (Gen 17:17).

Then pulling a serious face, but still in humorous vein, God challenged Abraham in a mock innocent tone: 'Why did Sarah laugh? Nothing is impossible for the Lord'. Whereupon, quickly sobering up in the presence of the Almighty, Sarah flatly denied that she had. 'Oh yes you did,' God insisted, at which point the original Jewish audience must have collapsed at the whole hilarious incident (Gen 18:13-15).

To cap it all, the perfect punch-line comes when the child is born and they call him Isaac which means in Hebrew, 'He laughs'!

The point of this humorous episode of course is that all things are possible to God. He was able give a child to an aged couple, and to found a chosen people from an old man as good as dead. He was also able to ensure the survival of that nation through every danger in their history.

Given the hardships of the Jews in the concentration camps of the Second World War, that message must still be very dear to their hearts. And for us, too, struggling against the dangers of sin, it is a source of great comfort to know that as Abraham's children in faith we are in God's protective hands. Nothing can harm us in a way that cannot be healed.

In the New Testament Jesus used his considerable wit to make this same point. Once when he was teaching the crowds about God's providential care as our Father, he noticed some men in the audience with their little children.

'Is there anyone among you,' he asked with a twinkle in his eye, 'who would hand his son a stone if he asked for bread? Or would hand him a snake when he asked for a fish? Or, if he asked for an egg, would hand him a scorpion?' (Mt 7:8-9; Lk 11:11-12). No group of men could have heard these words without a hearty guffaw. The very idea was ridiculous!

It is just as ridiculous to imagine that God could refuse any good thing to us, his children, if we ask him. As in our own day, Jesus knew that a serious message is often better received when delivered with a touch of light-heartedness.

Then there was the time the Canaanite woman ran after him with a request, hoping that what he had said to the men was true (Mt 15:21-28). At first, Jesus pretended not to notice her. Then he said surprisingly, 'It is not fair to take the children's food and throw it to little dogs'. She was a pagan, not one of the Jewish people to whom Jesus was primarily sent.

His reply might sound a bit cruel but in fact it wasn't. He was teasing her to draw out her faith. Not a bit offended or deterred, the woman recognized the good-natured taunt, and gave back as good as she got. 'Ah yes, Lord,' came her quick-thinking riposte, 'but even little dogs eat the scraps that fall from their masters' table'. Jesus had met his match! How could he not have laughed loudly after that, as he granted her what she wanted.

So the Lord is no dried-up poker-face. Nor does he want us to be poker-faced either. From the stories in Scripture, he's telling us very clearly that those who know how to laugh with God also know how to trust him. And there's no kidding about the importance of that.

14

Beneath Pain's Dark Surface

When you read in the papers about a major tragedy you may sometimes wonder why God allowed it to happen. The Jews of Jesus' time wondered about this too. They put it down to a punishment for sin.

On one occasion a tower collapsed on a crowd in the busy Siloam district of Jerusalem. Eighteen people were killed. All who heard about it simply supposed that these people had been more wicked than most, that this was their wickedness falling upon them.

In another instance the northern province of Galilee was stunned by Pilate's horrible massacre of a number of men whose blood he mingled with the sacrifices. These men, concluded the wise Jewish rabbis, were evidently great evil-doers whose sin was hidden from all but God alone. But Jesus didn't see it that way at all.

When he was told of these tragedies, Jesus dismissed any suggestion that the victims were being paid back by God for something they had done wrong. 'Do you suppose that these Galileans were worse sinners than any others,' he asked, 'that this should have happened to them? They were not, I tell you. Or those eighteen on whom the tower at Siloam fell, killing them all? Do you suppose that they were more guilty than all the other people living in Jerusalem? They were not, I tell you' (Lk 13:2-5).

This was a new teaching, a radical departure from traditional thinking. It must have greatly cheered Jesus' first disciples who were traditional Jews in their outlook. For us, too, Jesus' words bring a great relief because sometimes we can mistakenly suppose that misfortunes befall us because we have displeased God by our sins. Such a view only adds to suffering and causes despair.

For example a child is born handicapped and the mother thinks, 'What have I done to deserve this?' A close relative dies and we worry, 'Is this a punishment for my not taking more time to care?' An illness strikes and the idea occurs, 'Now God is getting even for the waywardness of my youth'. Let Christ's assurance be our consolation. God permits suffering, but does not inflict it.

St John's Gospel devotes an entire chapter to this point. Passing by a man blind from birth, the disciples ask the Lord, 'Rabbi, who sinned, this man or his parents, that he should have been born blind?' Jesus' answer is the same as before. 'Neither he nor his parents sinned,' he replies, 'he was born blind so that the works of God might be revealed in him' (Jn 9:1-3).

To debunk their myth, Jesus restores the man's sight by anointing his eyes with spittle. At the same time, he removes the blindness of his soul, and gives him the gift of faith in the Son of Man. In doing this, Jesus caused the Pharisees, who were standing by and who didn't believe in him, to ask themselves some questions. Who are the really blind in this world? Who are the ones who really see? Those who have good eyesight but no faith, or those who can see with the eyes of faith, even if their physical eyes are frail? (Jn 9: 35-41).

This incident is a wonderful example of how God can draw great blessings out of personal disablement. He does the same again today, if we permit him. One reason why he doesn't prevent suffering is that he knows how to turn it to the good.

This is what happened on Calvary. There God himself endured the most brutal agony of mind, body and spirit, and yet through the cross became the redemption of sinners. Although totally innocent of blame, Jesus accepted the capital punishment that our sins deserved. That sentence cancelled our crime so totally that there is no further penalty to be paid. Any pain that we endure therefore only brings us closer to God, because it unites us with Christ crucified.

If pain is to be something positive for us we have to believe that it conceals the glory of God beneath its dark surface. Even when this is hard to see, it is still true. At such times we should ask God to strengthen our faith in the cross, to help us believe, as St Paul says, that 'God works with those who love him... and turns everything to their good' (Rom 8:28). For he assures us, 'nothing shall separate us from the love of Christ, neither tribulation, nor distress, nor persecution, nor famine, nor nakedness, nor peril nor the sword... We come through all these things triumphantly victorious, by the power of him who loved us' (Rom 8:35-37).

15

The Silence of God

The other day I heard about someone who stopped praying because he asked God for something and didn't get it. It's a pity he didn't wait a bit. Maybe God had something better in store for him than what he was asking for.

People do get upset when God gives the silent response to prayer. They imagine he hasn't heard them, that they're wasting their time. Nothing could be further from the truth. God always hears our petitions and always answers them, even if the answer has to be 'No'.

Jesus assures us that when we ask in his name we receive. That's the gospel truth. Jesus cannot lie. How then are we to interpret his silence when, taking him at his word, we pray for help with exams, or a job interview, or money, or the right partner in life, or an end to a problem, and things do not turn out as we had hoped? Well, there are several reasons why we sometimes hear nothing, as we discover when we examine the silence of Jesus in the Scriptures.

Jesus was silent before Herod at his trial, for example (Lk 23:8-12). Although Herod was 'very glad when he saw Jesus, for he had long desired to see him, since he had heard about him and desired to see some sign done by him', yet Jesus made no answer to his questions. Silence was his only response. Herod's interest in the Lord was purely superficial; what other response could he expect?

Similarly with us. If our communication with God is superficial, based only on self-interest and not concerned with the Lord and his will, how can we hope to get the answer we want? God is not an automatic dispensing machine, producing the goods for a fifty-pence piece.

Jesus was silent with his friends too on occasion. One time when they were all in the boat, a great storm arose that threatened to sink them (Mk 4:35-41). Although they cried out in despair, Jesus didn't say a word. He was in fact asleep.

When they shook him awake, all he said to them was, 'O men of little faith, why were you afraid?' In other words, did they not know that they were perfectly safe with him on board, that nothing could harm them when he was present?

Maybe that's what he means us to hear too when our prayer is one of great anguish and he seems to be asleep on us. In such cases we need to ask ourselves how strong our belief in his peaceful presence really is; for that presence surrounds the daily lives of those who trust in him.

Even the great apostle Paul knew what it was like to pray hard for something important, only to receive a bewildering 'engaged tone'. No one in the New Testament had a stronger faith than he; no one worked harder than he for God's Kingdom on earth; yet even he had to come to grips with God's silence.

He tells us (2 Cor 12:7-10) that he was given 'a thorn in the flesh, a messenger of Satan to harass me'. What exactly this 'thorn in the flesh' was he doesn't say. Perhaps it was a physical ailment, or maybe a nervous affliction, or a spiritual weakness.

Three times he besought the Lord about this 'that it should leave me'. Evidently he got no satisfaction after the first and second petition. But on the third appeal, the Lord said to him, 'My grace is sufficient for you, for my power is made perfect in weakness'. In other words, there are things which God sees fit to leave weighing on our shoulders because, as Paul himself recognized, they make us humble. They make us realize our need for God's grace and our dependence on him.

Sometimes with us it's the same. There are certain

difficulties in life that make us turn to God and declare our need for him. They ensure that we pray always and stay close to him. Perhaps if we did not have them, we wouldn't pray at all.

St Ignatius of Antioch says that 'only the person who has mastered the words of Jesus can apprehend his silences'. If we truly listen to the gospel meditatively we will eventually – like St Paul – come to understand all that Jesus is saying to us, even in those moments of prayer when it seems that he has stopped saying anything at all.

16

Things Jesus Didn't Say

always feel slightly shocked when I read in St Luke's Gospel the words Jesus spoke to his friend Martha (Lk 10:38-42). 'Martha, Martha,' he said, 'you worry and fret about so many things, and yet few are needed, indeed only one. It is Mary who has chosen the better part, and it is not to be taken from her.'

After all, it was for Jesus that Martha was preparing the meal and she was getting precious little help from her sister Mary or from anyone else either. 'Lord,' she had complained earlier, 'do you not care that my sister is leaving me to do the serving all by myself? Please tell her to help me.' And where was Mary as Martha stirred the pot, set the table and rushed to have the first course ready? Sitting relaxed at the Lord's feet, listening to him speaking.

Did Martha take Jesus' remark as a slap in the face, an ungenerous response to the considerable trouble she was taking to offer him hospitality? We shall never know for sure for the Gospel doesn't tell us. But it seems unlikely because later when her brother Lazarus died, Jesus was the first one she ran to for consolation and help. We must presume that Martha had thought about what Jesus really meant, and had come to see that he was not belittling her good work in the kitchen. I'm sure he tucked in with relish to the marvellous dinner that eventually appeared!

What Jesus actually chided Martha for was her attitude. 'You *worry* and *fret* about so many things,' he said to her. Had the situation of the two sisters been reversed, had it been Mary who fretted as she sat at his feet, and Martha who served serenely, he might well have addressed his comment to Mary. What Jesus was saying was this: whether we are working or praying, it is the state of the heart that impresses him most. To be at peace is to be open to his presence; to be preoccupied and anxious is to stop trusting.

This wasn't the only time Jesus came out with a statement that caused a hush. One day when he was teaching his disciples his mother arrived and, waiting outside the house, asked to speak with him (Mt 12:46-50). To the man who brought in the message Jesus said, 'Who is my mother? Anyone who does the will of my Father in heaven is my brother and sister and mother'. It was enough to make them hold their breath. Was this not a slight to the Virgin Mary who had consented to become his mother, who had nourished him from infancy with deep affection, and who would stand by him at the cross on Calvary? No. It was in fact a compliment to her faithfulness, for more than anyone else Mary was one who carried out the Father's will to perfection.

Jesus was presenting his mother as a model of excellence, promising that those who did as she did would be loved as much as she was. Even if the others did not fully understand this at the time, there can be no doubt that Mary did, for she pondered all his sayings and treasured them in her heart.

The three people we have thought about – the Virgin Mary, Martha and her sister Mary – are models for all of us who read Scripture in private prayer and who listen to it on Sundays at Mass. They teach us how to interpret the words of the Lord correctly. It is so easy to misinterpret them or to impose a meaning on them that was never intended. When we come across a passage that sounds difficult or even outrageous the temptation is to let it go, or to jump to the first conclusion that suggests itself. This is not what the Lord intended. He sometimes chooses to put things in an odd way in order to make us think, to shock us out of our complacency, or to convey the urgency of his message. If the word of God means anything to us we will accept the challenge it offers, allowing it to mature in our hearts the way new wine is left to mature. The longer it lies the better it ferments; the more slowly it is sipped, the richer it tastes.

17

Playing Second Fiddle

One character in the Gospels I admire is Andrew the Apostle. Brother to Simon Peter – Christ's chosen henchman and leader of the Twelve – Andrew must have felt dwarfed in the shadow of his brother's gigantic reputation. For every occurrence of Andrew's name in Scripture, Peter's is mentioned twenty times. In fact the incidents involving Andrew are so few they could be written down on the back of an envelope, whereas you could write a book about Peter from the wealth of information we have on him.

And yet there is no indication that Andrew ever showed any jealousy over his brother's fame or his own supporting role as second fiddle. This is surprising really when you consider how most of us react when unfavourably compared with others.

For example youngsters hate to be compared with older brothers or sisters who have done well at school or in sport. In a radio interview I heard a writer who had published a best-seller late in life confess that she had written it to steal the limelight from her even more celebrated sibling. She resented, she said, always being introduced as somebody else's sister, and craved to be appreciated for her own worth alone.

Not so with Andrew. On the three occasions when he appears in the Gospel, it is always to bring someone else to Jesus' notice and then to retire quietly into the background himself.

It was Andrew who first brought Peter and Jesus together (Jn 1:35-42). By the river Jordan he had heard John the

Baptist proclaim Jesus to be the Lamb of God. Having discovered Jesus for himself, he hurried off to tell his brother that he had met the Messiah. Then he took him back to Jesus, introduced him, and moved to one side. He didn't boast that he had met Jesus first. Nor was there any bitterness because his brother received the keys to the kingdom of heaven instead of him!

The second person Andrew brought to Jesus was the little boy with the five loaves and two fish (Jn 6:5-15). There was a crowd of five thousand with them on that occasion and they were starving. What use was so little food among so many? Andrew didn't worry about that. He simply presented what was available through the hands of the child, and let Jesus work out a solution to the problem. It takes faith and humility to do that. Andrew had plenty of both.

On the third occasion, some Greeks came looking for Jesus in Jerusalem during the feast of the Jewish Passover (Jn 12:20-28). They ran into Philip and explained why they had come. So what did Philip do? He brought them to Andrew! Obviously Andrew was noted among the Apostles for his success in making introductions that bore fruit.

Together they led the Greeks to Christ, and at that moment Jesus announced his hour had come to suffer and die for the redemption of the world. It was as if the arrival of these foreigners had given Jesus some hidden signal that the new Passover was about to begin. Once again Andrew's humble and retiring performance should merit him an award as 'best supporting actor'!

Today many of us tend to want credit for any good we do. Sometimes we kick up a fuss or sulk if we don't get it. What's even worse, we often make others pay for the good turn we do them by reminding them about it and embarrassing them, or by making them feel indebted to us.

Clearly this drains charity out of our good deeds. To put charity back in again, the self must be drained out instead. Then the good we do will be really good, because it will cause others to meet and love the Christ within us. As in the past, so in the present, Jesus still waits expectantly to see who are his Andrews today and whom they will bring to him in the Church of the new millennium.

20

A Sign of God's Fidelity

esus worked his first miracle at a wedding reception. According to St John's Gospel he changed water into wine to spare the bridal couple embarrassment and disappointment on their wedding day. Their married life was not going to start with a sense of failure if he had any thing to do with it. St John called it 'the first of his signs' and noted that it caused his disciples to believe in him (Jn 2:11). A sign is a thing that points to something like itself. So what did this unusual miracle signify?

It signified that Jesus has the power to change the quality of human love. Love is so precious in God's eyes, he wishes it to last. For this to happen it has to be transformed. Jesus wanted the young couple's life together to be a success from start to finish. It had to be more than a matter of water; he wanted to turn it into a sparkling wine. And that is one reason why his disciples believed in him – they recognized what the miracle meant.

They knew as Jesus did that natural affection, no matter how strong, is fragile. That it needs to be protected in a world that is often hostile to fidelity, commitment and self-giving – the very things that support a relationship. These are qualities however that demand sacrifice, and there has always been a trend that despises self-sacrifice. It wasn't fashionable in their day and it isn't fashionable now. Yet without discipline, vigilance and care, the tenderness in love goes out of it, evaporates like morning mist. Jesus could not bear to think of that happening to the marriage at which he was an invited guest.

He was also aware that good intentions are not enough, that even the best efforts of husbands and wives on their own do not guarantee a stable partnership. For that, it requires the touch of God himself. Therefore he wanted to make God present in every union, as he himself was present that day in Galilee.

That's why he worked his first miracle at a nuptial feast. He had a message for married couples before he had a message for any one else. 'I can fill your boat with wine', he wanted to tell them. And it was true. He did not produce merely a litre of *vino rosso* at Cana; he produced a deluge.

'There were six stone water jars standing there', recounts St John, 'each holding twenty or thirty gallons'. The banquet was flowing with it, a fine, full-bodied, fruit-filled vintage, according to the *maitre d'hotel* who was thoroughly astonished at the quality! Enough grace in fact to make it a marriage to remember, to give it substance, to make it holy.

But Jesus had another reason for holding marriage sacred. He saw in it a sign of his Father's yearning for his people. The Old Testament prophets were forever likening Yahweh's relationship with Israel to a husband's desire for his wife. Isaiah for example thought of him as a young man intoxicated with love and not afraid to show it.

'As a young man marries a virgin', he told his listeners, 'so shall the Lord marry you. And as the bridegroom rejoices over the bride, so will your God rejoice over you' (Is 62:5).

Because of this Jesus made matrimony a sacrament. The sacraments are the living signs of God's inexhaustible fidelity. They prove him incapable of breaking his vows. After Jesus, every sacramental marriage is a miracle that points to unbreakable love. Yes a miracle, given that human beings themselves are so breakable. And yet in their married life they make the divine love present in a human way, a constant reminder to the world of God's reliability, a reminder that no matter how things change, he does not.

Jesus' first miracle was to turn water into wine; his last was to change wine into his blood. At the table of the Last

Supper he passed the chalice into the hands of the same disciples who believed in him at Cana. 'Take this all of you and drink it,' he told them; 'this is the cup of the new covenant in my blood'.

It was another sign. It foreshadowed his death on the cross when he would open his arms in a spousal embrace and pour himself out for his bride the Church. Once again he had left the best wine to the last to show how seriously he took his own wedding and family life.

At that moment the miracle of Cana was made complete. Here was a power with which to build a life that would last. Poured into the chalice of matrimony and overflowing the brim, more than was needed, this was the essence of Christ himself, to enrich and transform what people are capable of and to make commitment into something extraordinary, especially in times of difficulty and challenge.

And that is why marriage and Eucharist have always been linked, as Jesus intended from the start. One sacrament draws strength from the other. When couples celebrate the Lord's Supper together their union is supported and fortified and revitalized. Holy Communion reinforces marital communion.

The miracle of the Eucharist repeats the miracle of Cana. It reproduces it in the miracle of the cross. And every time this happens God renews his whole Church, brings his own bride closer to himself. He does so through the witness of those couples in whom his love has come to rest and to ferment and to mature.

19

Ten Little Lepers

hen some evil befalls us the chances are we will say nothing about it for a while at least, until we see how things progress. But when that evil passes, the relief is so great we cannot but speak of it. Joy is such an uncontainable force, it bursts out in spite of us! To be able to express it is often a fulfilment or completion of the good experience. It is indeed part of the healing of the original pain that has now passed.

I expect such joy is really a rendering of thanks and praise to God, the source of all healing relief, and joyfulness. And the way it is expressed is through our telling someone else the whole story from the beginning. How the anxiety grew at first, the trouble it caused, then the turning-point when it was no longer a threat and finally the realization that there was nothing to be concerned about any more.

Many people in the gospels went through just what I am talking about. Those who were physically or psychologically healed by Jesus. The paralytic in the second chapter of Mark, for example; the parents of the little girl whom Christ raised from death (Mk 5); the demoniac possessed by a legion of delinquent spirits (Mk 5).

In a lot of these cases Jesus actually asked them not to say anything about their healing. He did not want the crowds to come and make him king. But he was wasting his breath. St Mark tells us that after curing a man who was both deaf and dumb, 'the more Jesus charged them to say nothing, the more zealously they proclaimed it' (7:36).

You can understand why. How could they keep such a thing to themselves? They had witnessed the love of God in Christ for a poor man, had seen for themselves what an effect such love can have. The incident moved them to immediate faith in Jesus. Their joy overflowed.

Because joy cannot contain itself, they told the story far and wide. After Jesus' resurrection the apostolic Church did the same. It preached the good news at home and abroad through sheer inability to keep it quiet. The telling made it complete (1 Jn 1:4). It was the ultimate remedy for dispelling the bad news they had experienced before Jesus came – the despair of ever breaking free from sin and death, the anguish of being at odds with God no matter how much they tried. Spreading the message was the natural sign of their deep appreciation of what God had done for them in Jesus whose healing power touched the soul as well as the body.

The disciples knew that those outward healings were a sign of something becoming whole again underneath. Christ was more than just a good physician; he was the Saviour. What he brought was much more valuable than medical help – for we all die eventually. It was the salve of eternal life, given here and now to all who are ready to receive it.

On one occasion however some who were healed forgot to be joyful. The nine lepers failed to tell their wonderful story. They can't have had much faith in the first place. And one wonders what happened to them afterwards. They are never mentioned again. They exit from the story of the gospel as suddenly as they entered.

There were ten of them altogether. Excluded from society because of their disease – like AIDS victims today – they had to stand at a distance when any one passed. Then they saw Jesus. All they could do was call to him from afar. The Law prevented them from drawing near.

Jesus was moved to the depths of his pity. 'Go and show yourselves to the priest,' he said – the custom when a leper had recovered. As they set off their flesh became whole again: they were cured. However only one came back. Falling on his knees he thanked Jesus aloud, praising God at the top of his voice, telling his story to all creation. Jesus was looking sadly into the distance. Where were the other nine? Did they not have a story to tell too? 'Go in peace,' Jesus said to the man at his feet, 'your faith makes your healing complete'.

What faith? Not just the original belief which made him call out when he was ill. But the faith he now displayed as he acknowledged Jesus' goodness aloud. It was his uninhibited gratitude for the gracious favour shown him that restored him to health in spirit as well as body, and kept him sound.

It is important that we tell our story too if we want to remain whole in Christ. He heals us every time we ask, forgiving our sins and imperfections; helping us repair broken relationships; moving us to repent of stubborn ways; enabling us make changes to improve our response to the Gospel; keeping us on the straight and narrow when we teeter at the edge. And in a million other ways known to each of us alone. But if we keep it to ourselves and fail to celebrate, going off like the nine on the road away from Christ, we will lose contact with the *source* of our healing and end up sadder than before.

We tell our story first of all in prayer: by going to Mass and acknowledging grace publicly through our presence there; by expressing gratitude privately in personal prayer as well. We tell it equally by our actions – by avoiding occasions of past sin and making conscious efforts to cultivate good habits. Sometimes we tell our story in words to another person or group: at a prayer meeting perhaps, or to someone in need of spiritual encouragement. By doing so we complete the healing Christ gives us through faith.

If we never tell our tale in some of these ways, the chances are we have not really been cured in the first place.

A Little Touch of Faith

Most of the miracles recorded of Jesus in the New Testament are very deliberate acts on his part. He sees a need, addresses it, then does whatever is necessary for the person concerned. But there is one case where the healing happened even before Jesus knew who it was. It is one of the most interesting events in the Bible.

The reason Jesus was unaware of the healing is twofold. First he was in a rush; on his way to the bedside of a little girl who was seriously ill. In fact she died before he arrived. So his mind was on that at the time. Secondly, he was in the middle of a throng of people heaving and swelling around him, jostling and bumping him, like Regent Street on a Saturday afternoon. And that distracted him as well.

Suddenly he stopped in his tracks. 'Somebody has touched my garments,' he said. And he would not move till he found out who. The disciples were amazed at him. 'You see the crowd pressing round you,' they protested, wondering what had come over him, 'and yet you say, "Who touched me?"' However despite the emergency he stood his ground and waited.

He was right. Someone had touched him from behind. Not like others who knocked into him indifferently as people do in a crowd. This person had reached out to him deliberately, had reverently held the hem of his cloak, the little fringe actually that decorated the edges. Then just as quietly she slipped away again into the busy crowd and disappeared.

How did Jesus know something had happened? Because, says Mark's Gospel (5:30), he felt power for healing go out of him. Automatically. Such is the nature of God. The moment faith stretches out its hand to him, virtue is released even before he can stop it! And Jesus was determined to find the person who knew that.

But did it matter who she was? Especially since he was needed by a child close to death? Yes, it did. This woman had not only touched his garments; she had also touched his heart. Anyone who had faith like that, he wanted to meet. Such trust, he felt, deserved a personal response from him; it deserved his friendship. He wanted to affirm this woman's faith, acknowledge what she had done.

Without the personal, one-to-one encounter with him, she might think that touching relics is more important than knowledge of God. Or that belief can be sustained without talking to him. For her to vanish without finding out how he cared for her faith would have grieved him. And so he put every other case to one side till she came back.

And when she did he told her, 'It was your faith that healed you', not the fringe of the garment. He called her, 'Daughter', and bade her, 'Go in peace', and then he pronounced the words that made her cure complete, 'Be healed of your disease'. It had been an internal bleeding that had lasted twelve years. An embarrassing complaint, deeply painful, deeply personal. His gentle tone showed understanding and kindness. It also healed her self-respect, her femininity.

And so with us, implies St Mark. Prayer to God means relationship with Christ. Real faith means daily discipleship. Reaching out to him means you don't run away. You stay. For while God always answers the need of the moment he wants us to want something more, namely himself. Faith may move mountains, but love conquers God. For the sake of that love, Christ would stand still in a crowd and wait for ever.

So what about the child who died while Jesus delayed? She wasn't able to reach him like the woman did. No problem. He went to her in his own good time and simply raised her from the dead.

21

Gradual Improvement

Of all the healing miracles Jesus performed, the one I find easiest to imagine – because most like nature's own way of healing – is that of the blind man in Mark's Gospel, chapter 8. It is quite different from any of the other miracle because of the *way* it was done.

Instead of curing the man's blindness all at once, Jesus did it in stages. Leading him by the hand out of the village where he lived, Christ put spittle on his eyes and then asked, 'Do you see any thing?' 'I see men,' replied the man looking up, 'but they look like trees walking'. So Jesus touched his eyes once more. The blind man stared intently; this time he could see perfectly. Sight was fully restored.

From blindness to blurred vision, from a blur to clear sightedness. You can almost envisage it happening. Something in the gradual change rings true. Like going to the optician to get your glasses changed.

But it is an unusual miracle as gospel miracles go. It is as if we were meant to see something beyond the actual story. So what is Mark trying to show us?

Mainly that Jesus is not just a good optician but the Light. Everything he did pointed to a gift of deeper significance. In this case, *insight*. How many people see Jesus as the Son of God for example? Or perceive what that actually means?

Interestingly, in the passage immediately after the cure of the blind man Jesus asks his own disciples – Simon Peter and the Eleven – 'Who do you say that I am?' In other words, though I may be familiar to you by sight do you recognize who I really am and what I have come to do? The question is directed to everyone. Which is why Mark places it in the centre of his Gospel. It is a question of central importance, the most important one ever asked for upon the answer depends our salvation.

Simon Peter knew the correct answer readily enough: 'You are the Christ', but he didn't see what that involved. At least not at first. He had to come to it gradually. Like the man with the blurred vision. Short-sighted, so that everyone looked like trees walking. Even when Jesus tried to explain that this tree was the cross, that the Christ had to suffer and in that way heal the blindness of sin, Peter did not want to look.

'God forbid, Lord! This shall never happen to you', is what he actually said according to Matthew's version of the same incident (16:22). Had Peter succeeded in dissuading Jesus from his passion, the world's night would still be unredeemed.

To acknowledge the cross in Christ is to share it with him. Maybe that is why Peter tried to talk him out of it. He did not want to get that close to suffering.

But Jesus did not smudge the truth; he made it crystal clear to all the disciples. 'If anyone would come after me, let him deny himself and take up his cross and follow me.' Not till later did Peter see the point. And so on Good Friday he disappeared, was nowhere to be seen.

However, when the shadow of Calvary gave way to the light of Easter his vision changed. The experience of resurrection opened the eyes of his faith fully, enabled him to accept his own crucifixion three decades later at the Vatican hill in Rome. The gradual healing was complete.

Most interesting of all in Mark's Gospel is the way the story comes back to the blind man theme after Jesus' question to Peter. For in the following chapter he describes the cure of the blind beggar, Bartimaeus, but concludes this incident in a way that is different from the other one.

'Your faith has made you well,' Jesus said to the beggar, now sighted; and immediately, Mark adds, 'he followed

Jesus on the road' (10:52). Followed him, that is, as his disciple along the path to his death. Jesus had bestowed on him more than physical vision. He had given him spiritual insight too. Whoever possesses this, Mark seems to be showing us, becomes capable of going anywhere with Jesus.

When we shirk the suffering that comes from following Jesus, flinch at the pain involved in being faithful to his teaching; when we cringe at the inconvenience of obeying his word, or wish for a different cross than the one he has laid upon us, we should not despair. The miracle of faith is just not yet complete in us. Gradually, for those who truly desire it, the patient hands of Christ will touch our eyes a second time. Then, as with Peter or Bartimaeus, or the blind man of Mark, chapter 8, we will recognize the glory of the cross as well as its darkness because we will see that Jesus carries it with us and is leading us through it to the blessed vision of the Father.

22

A Christic for Troubled Times

Jesus performed his most dramatic miracle one bitter night when he braved a wild and wind-swept sea to walk across its waters. The story appears again and again in the New Testament (Mt 14; Mk 6; Jn 6), so it meant a lot to the early Christian Churches. It still has a lot to say to us who live in troubled times today. Vicious, squally storms are common enough on the Sea of Galilee. The wind from the surrounding hills gets trapped in the saucer of the lake below and it takes a while to blow itself out again. Any hapless little craft out on such a night will find itself in serious difficulty without warning. Even experienced boatmen can find themselves caught in the terror of these sudden tempests.

This is what happened to the disciples. They were rowing across to Bethsaida when, three or four miles out from land, the wind descended on them like a hawk and savaged the waves around them. They had left Jesus behind on the other shore. He had wanted to go to the hills by himself to pray and so they were alone. They started to panic.

They must have struggled all night with the storm because Mark tells us they set out before evening and were still in trouble by 'the fourth watch of the night' that is by four or five in the morning. To understand what they went through, ask any fisherman from the West of Ireland about the sea at night. He will tell you better than I of the despair that swamps even the stoutest hearts.

When the gale was at its worst, when the boat was ready to go under, when the men were about to give up, Jesus came to them walking on the sea. They saw him and were petrified. 'Do not be afraid!' he called to them in a calm voice, 'It is I' (Jn 6). 'Take heart, it is I; have no fear' (Mk 6; Mt 14). Then he climbed into the boat beside them and that was it. The wind dropped, the waves died down, the storm ceased. Before they knew it they were at the other side, the crisis had passed.

What makes this such a fascinating story is that it is not just about a storm at sea. It is about Jesus' power to tread underfoot every trauma that threatens to destroy people. When he rose from the tomb on Easter morning he put his foot on everything that makes us despair and shattered it.

Indeed some scripture scholars insist that the walking on the waters was one of the resurrection appearances, that it happened after Easter, that the gospel writers inserted it early in the narrative to alert their readers to who Jesus really was and what he had power to do.

Why might they have done this? To reassure the struggling Christian communities of the first century AD who were facing enormous problems as they tried to live the gospel and share it with others: opposition from the Jewish authorities, persecution from the Romans, power struggles in their own ranks, personal sinfulness wave upon wave of challenge and trial, year in year out!

Yet the Church's strength, the evangelists reminded them, is the living Christ in their midst. Even though he had ascended to the Father, he was still with them. Having risen above these things himself, he was showing *them* how to rise above things too so that they should not be overwhelmed, no matter how dark the night or turbulent the gale.

Did this mean Jesus wished to protect his disciples from reality? Was the gospel suggesting the Church should anaesthetize itself against crises and difficulties until they simply went away? Hardly. Jesus did not anaesthetize himself against reality on the cross at Calvary. He even refused the painkiller of wine and myrrh offered to deaden the agony of his dying.

Nor does the gospel propose running away from the cross of daily living. Quite the opposite. Unless the cross is taken up and shouldered every morning, no person can be a follower of Christ.

What the walking on the waters does teach us is that when people do their best to contend with the storm, the Easter Jesus will not abandon them. As Lord of the resurrection he will come to them in person and bring their efforts to completion. He will get into the boat with them and bless their journey with his peace.

Therefore there is no need to be afraid of failure; there is never any justification for despair. Hopelessness is out of harmony with faith. It would be an inappropriate response to the situation. Even when the storm lasts all night, even when Jesus is on a different shore, disciples do not give up. Christ is in the hills praying for his Church. He has the boat constantly in view. He is himself Master of the wind and sea. He will make his appearance in his own good time.

It is interesting that Matthew, Mark and John preface the calming of the storm with the feeding of the five thousand, when Jesus provided the multitudes of his followers with bread in abundance. It was a sign of the Eucharist which was to come later. The evangelists unanimously link the two incidents. First the provision of bread, then the walking through the storm. First the Eucharist, then the victory over the hurricane. First the Bread of Life, then the encounter with the risen Lord.

In Mark's account the evangelist even underlines the connection: 'After Jesus got into the boat and the wind dropped they were utterly and completely dumbfounded, because they had not seen what the miracle of the loaves meant; their minds were closed' (6:51-52).

What were their minds were closed to? The Eucharist as Sacrament of Peace. The Lord who has the power to change bread into his risen body is a Lord who is worthy of trust. Transforming all things in himself, he not only turns darkness into light, turbulence into calm but also insecurity into confidence, agitation into serenity. And this is why he gently upbraided them for their lack of faith, and why the early Churches cherished this story.

So long as they celebrated the Eucharist they had all that was required to tackle trouble without anxiety. For through this sacrament Jesus would always be with them, unleashing the full force of his death and resurrection. Even in troubled times they knew there was no force in the universe greater than this.

Two thousand years later, history has proved them right. Christ is still nourishing the faith that proclaims him as Lord and that acknowledges his victory over the world. Jesus loves to walk on troubled waters and wishes not to walk alone!

23

A Question of Healing

For anyone who has been on pilgrimage to Lourdes, there is one miracle of Jesus in the Gospel (Jn chapter 5) they should find very easy to visualise: the healing of the man at the pool of Bethzatha. Bethzatha was an area in the North East of Jerusalem near the Sheep Gate. The pool was said to have curative properties so it was thronged with the sick who flocked there to find a remedy for their illnesses.

Some think the name Bethzatha may mean *House of Mercy*, so called because of the building nearby set up to accommodate the elderly, the lame, the paralysed and the blind who were laid out on stretchers in the porticoes that surrounded the pool. Others say it means *Place of the Double Gusher*, because of the two-fold drain that fed the pool from the natural spring at its source. Every now and then this spring would suddenly become active, causing the water to bubble. It was believed that the first person in when this happened would be restored to health.

Archaeologists have found the remains of this ancient site. It is near the Church of St Anne. They discovered the ruins of a four-sided double cistern intersected by a dividing wall. They also found the base of five colonnades that once supported the five porticoes mentioned in St John's account, where the crippled and ailing were placed.

Probably there was a system of helpers at Bethzatha, as there is at Lourdes today, to facilitate the patients when the water began to move. They would ease the disabled into the pool and keep order in the queue. In all likelihood those who could afford it brought their own helpers to look after them when their turn came.

One patient was there who had no one to put him in. As he said himself, 'I have no man to put me into the pool when the water is troubled, and while I am going down another steps down before me'. He had been a sufferer for thirty-eight years and Jesus knew – as he passed by that day – he had been waiting there for a very long time.

Given this fact, the question he asked him was a curious one. 'Do you want to be healed?' Curious because you would imagine the answer was pretty obvious. Why else would he have gone so often to the pool of healing? Why do people go to Lourdes? Or to the doctor? Or to a counsellor or psychiatrist?

Beneath Jesus' question lies a bubbling spring of wisdom and insight.

Are there some illnesses people do not really want to get over? Take the man in the Gospel for instance. Could it be he was quite comfortable in his disablement? Might this have been his way of opting out of life? Did he enjoy being dependent on others, not having to face the responsibilities of caring for anyone but himself? Did he like to feel sorry for himself, like to feel abandoned, to feel pitied?

It is interesting that it was Jesus who approached him rather than he who called on Jesus – as so many others did in the New Testament. After thirty-eight years had he given up praying? Did he think it was too late to be made right again, that life had already passed him by?

Whatever the answer to these questions, Jesus said to him, 'Rise, take up your pallet and walk', and at once he was healed and walked. No dip in the pool was needed, the personal encounter with Christ was enough.

His specific illness is not named. It may have been paralysis, some spinal disorder, crippled feet or a defect from birth. Whatever it was it kept him down, immobile. His main problem seems to have been that he had no one to help him. This was the only disadvantage he complained of. Perhaps he was too poor to hire a helper.

In Christ he found a man to help. God-made-man. The incarnate Son of the Father. 'My Father is working still,' Jesus said later by way of explanation, 'and I am working'. Through the humanity of Jesus the divine love of God set this cripple on his feet, made him mobile, gave him heart, renewed his quality of life, restored his youth, brought him back to active community.

Many who go to Lourdes do not come back again healed of their physical infirmity. But almost all come back altered in outlook. They speak of a change of attitude – to life, to their illness, to themselves.

And that is truly miraculous. To be lifted up in one's spirit out of depression and hopelessness, to be relieved of the sense of uselessness infirmity often causes, is real healing. Whether we are disabled or not, what matters is how we cope. Being healthy does not in itself bring happiness – frequently people who are physically well are miserable.

What counts is finding a purposefulness to life, a way of turning disadvantage into an opportunity for good, a way of expressing what is good in our personality: compassion towards others, a sense of humour, an optimism that is healthy and fresh and infectious, and youthful and vital and flowing with hope.

'My Father is working in you still,' Jesus is continually saying today through the Gospel, 'and I am working. Do you want to be healed? Then take up your life and walk'.

24

Lazarus

esus' first miracle was performed at a wedding; his last, just after a funeral. One of his closest friends had died at Bethany. Jesus was away at the time and did not attend the burial. He arrived four days later to pay his respects to the family, by which stage the body would have started to decompose behind the great stone that sealed its cave-like tomb.

Lazarus, the deceased, and his sisters Martha and Mary kept an open house for Jesus and his disciples. Situated two miles only from Jerusalem their home provided an ideal place to stay when Jesus was in the area. Particularly at Passover when Jerusalem was overrun with pilgrims and every available room was taken. The short walk to Bethany beyond the Mount of Olives was always a pleasant one at the end of the day when, tired after the ceremonies, they had a warm welcome awaiting them.

Martha would cook a good meal for her starving guests; Mary would sit and entertain, listening to Jesus with interest. And Lazarus, being the man of the house, would undoubtedly play the host in the best tradition of Jewish hospitality – washing their feet, serving the wine, organizing the seating at table. Many a wonderful supper was held in that home where the company was good, the conversation memorable and the laughter easy and loud.

But now Lazarus was dead. The marvellous get-togethers were over. How could such occasions be the same when one so loved was gone forever? And Jesus had not even been there. Where was he when he was so much needed? 'If Jesus had only been here,' said Martha, 'Lazarus would not have died!' She was quite sure of that. And Mary said the same. 'If Jesus had been here when Lazarus took ill...'. Had he not healed scores of sick people in his day? The blind, the paralysed, even the little girl who had died – he had raised her up before she had time to decompose. But it was too late for Lazarus. Four days he had lain in the bowels of the earth.

When Jesus eventually turned up, the sisters led him to the graveside. Overcome with the emotion of it all, he simply stood and cried for his friend in the tomb. John the Evangelist who was with him described it very poignantly in what is the shortest verse in the Bible: 'Jesus wept' (Jn 11:35).

At length he wiped his eyes. 'Take away the stone,' he said. Martha and Mary sobered up at once. The corpse would have started to smell. What was Jesus thinking of? 'Your brother,' he told them, 'is going to rise again'. 'Yes, Lord,' Martha replied with puzzled seriousness, 'I know he will rise again in the resurrection at the last day'. 'I am the resurrection', Jesus said affirmatively; 'Whoever believes in me, even though he dies, yet shall he live'. And in a loud voice that caused the throng of mourners to gasp, in a voice such as had never been heard since Eden, he roared into the dark hollow of the burial chamber, 'Lazarus, come out!'

The divine word of Life, angry and bitter with Death for thieving what belonged to the Creator, echoed through the underworld, reclaiming its stolen prize: 'Come out! Out! Out!'

And from the silent blackness of the tomb's yawning jaws, a touch of white appeared as Death regurgitated the contents of the grave. There stood Lazarus, swathed in the bleached binding-ribbons of his burial shroud, the linen napkin still covering his face. 'Unbind him,' ordered Jesus, 'and let him go.'

At the meal in Christ's honour that was held at Bethany later, Martha was ecstatic. 'Truly you are the Messiah,' she kept repeating and everyone agreed. A multitude was swarming round the door to catch a glimpse of Lazarus. The whole village had erupted. But Jesus was unusually quiet and Mary understood why.

To raise a man from the dead, a price has to be paid. Death was not to be cheated without a struggle. And the ministers of death – the Pharisees – were already taking counsel how best to destroy Jesus. With this latest public act he had gone too far. All Israel would soon be his disciples; then where would religion be? The temple, the laws, the customs of the Jews would simply disappear. It was time for the authorities to intervene. 'Far better', announced the High Priest, 'that one man should die for the people than that the whole nation should perish'. He spoke more prophetically than he realized.

It was nearly Jewish Passover, the time for sacrifice. Between Bethany and Bethlehem the fields were white with lambs for slaughter. The hungry grave would have its fill again – its last. Seeing what was to ensue, Mary produced a whole pound of the most expensive ointment she could buy and anointed Jesus' feet. She was preparing him in advance for his own funeral which would come upon him swiftly, leaving no time for the niceties of bereavement or the customary rites of respect.

What she did not know was what would happen later. Her joy at the raising of her brother was so full, she could not have guessed this was a sign of something even greater – the Easter mystery. She could not have recognized in it a promise to raise *everyone's* brother by the emptying of Jesus' tomb. For that is what it was.

And yet the resurrection of Christ was much more than what happened to Lazarus. Lazarus' body was merely resuscitated, restored to normal life, not resurrected. He would die again, be buried once more. On Easter Sunday morning Jesus' body was not resuscitated. It was transformed. The resurrection did not just happen to Jesus; Jesus is himself the resurrection: 'I am the resurrection and the life', as he told Martha at Lazarus' grave. And all who die in him believing in his power over death and sin, share in his human transformation too. What happens to us in the Easter experience is Jesus.

It begins with the raising of our spirits, out of depression and sadness and despair. It continues with the raising of our morale, in fresh hope and new opportunities for change. It will end with the complete raising of our lives to the Father in heaven – here and now through holiness of life, and hereafter in the beatific vision of the saints. So complete will the mystery be, it will involve every part of our being – the physical as well as the spiritual. In a manner no one can anticipate – any more than Martha or Mary could – it will leave us with identity intact yet free from the forces of evil that demean us. No longer subject to second death – as Lazarus' body was – we will be children of joy; our banquets will never again be overshadowed with the losing of the company we treasure.

Jesus' first miracle was performed at a wedding; his last, just after a funeral: his own. Following Easter, every day is a miracle of grace and eternal life. And even when these days are ended the miracle will continue, for being eternal that life belongs not to Death but to God – and to us.

25

The Play within the Play

hakespeare was very fond of the play within the play. A little drama enacted by different characters set at the turning point of the real drama for a particular purpose. Take *Hamlet* for instance. The Prince of Denmark suspects his uncle, Claudius, of murdering his father to win the throne and the Queen. He needs, however, to provoke a reaction that will make Claudius give himself away. So Hamlet stages a piece of theatre for the court's entertainment, and watches its effect.

The murder scene is re-enacted as the Prince believed it happened. In comes the villain while his victim is asleep in the garden. Claudius suddenly turns to Hamlet. 'What do you call the play?' he asks. 'The Mouse-trap', replies the other. The scene continues. The murderer pours the poison in the sleeper's ear. 'He poisons him in the garden for his estate,' explains Hamlet. 'You shall see anon how the murderer gets the love of (the victim's) wife.'

Claudius rises in fright and disappears. The trap has been sprung! The desired reaction has been provoked, the truth made public. The real play can now move to its own dramatic climax and tragic end.

Jesus was very fond of the play within the play too. Little theatrical stories set in the heart of the gospel that shed light on the gospel truth. We call them his parables. Extremely well-composed narratives with well-drawn characters, a clever story-line, and a surprising moral twist in the tail. All sketched in condensed language, simple words and pithy sentences that would be difficult to forget. So clear that a child could repeat the whole thing on one hearing; so profound in meaning that scripture scholars are still scrutinizing them today. And, like Hamlet's little play, designed to provoke a reaction in the listener that will reveal his heart. Take the parable of the Vineyard for example (Mt 21:33-46).

'A householder planted a vineyard, taking much trouble to make it fertile,' Jesus began. 'Then he let it to tenants who were so selfish that they withheld the fruit when the season for grapes came round.' There were chief priests and Pharisees in his audience. They were listening very carefully to this story.

'So the owner of the vineyard sent messengers to get his fruit. But the tenants beat them and stoned them.' The Pharisees stiffened. What was Jesus getting at? Was God the vineyard owner? Were the messengers his prophets? Could Israel be the vineyard, and the tenants be the Pharisees themselves? Their blood pressure rose.

'Finally he sent his son to them. "They will respect my son," he said.' Jesus glanced at the chief priests. 'But the wicked tenants said to themselves, "This is the heir. Come let us kill him and have his inheritance".' Now he paused and looked around at his listeners. 'When the vineyard owner comes,' he asked, 'what do you suppose he will do to those tenants?' The audience replied, 'He will put those wretches to a miserable death, and let out the vineyard to other tenants who will give him the fruits in their season.' Exactly!

In reporting this incident to us, St Matthew concludes: 'When the chief priests and the Pharisees heard his parables, they perceived that he was speaking about them. But when they tried to arrest him, they feared the multitudes, because they held him to be a prophet' (21:45-46).

Another mouse-trap had been sprung! The short story had produced the reaction intended, the hatred against Jesus was made public. Now the tragic course of the gospel could proceed to its inevitable end at Calvary.

Who says that stories are not dangerous? They are lethal!

They have killed God himself! They are also designed to bring about a death in us – the death of hypocrisy and pride and stubborn resistance to God's goodness. Jesus knew his stories would end in his death. The Pharisees feared his stories would end in the death of their tradition and privileges. Maybe those who turn away from the Gospel today also shirk the death to one's self that it requires and the change to one's life that must happen if the story is taken seriously.

Literary critics sometimes argue that maybe Hamlet was mad. Perhaps he imagined it all: his duty to his father, Claudius' guilt, his mother's infidelity in marrying again so soon. What he took as Claudius' self-betrayal – could it not simply have been that the uncle realized his nephew was insane and withdrew from his play within the play on that account? The question remains a moot point.

They said the same about Jesus. Even his relatives were convinced he was mad (Mk 3:21). Only a mad man would put his head in the noose by telling the tales that he told, surely?

If Jesus was not mad, then it means that most around him were. It raises the question, doesn't it, who are the foolish and who are the wise? St Paul had no doubt in his mind as to the answer. 'The foolishness of God,' he wrote to the Corinthians, 'is wiser than the wisdom of men. And the weakness of God is stronger than men's strength' (1 Cor 1:25). Yes Jesus was foolish enough to take a risk and lost his life over it.

But go back to his parable again and see! The vineyard which is the Kingdom of God has been taken from those tenants who failed to produce the fruit and has been given to us, the rest of the world, the 'other tenants', so that we may produce the fruits of salvation.

Had Jesus not been rejected by his own people, we would have been lost. But because of his death we are saved. And when the whole world has been evangelized, adds St Paul, the Jews will be drawn into the Kingdom as well, so that God's plan will be realized in and through Christ Jesus.

And there's the difference between *Hamlet* and the Gospel. *Hamlet* ended in tragedy, the Gospel does not. Whether he was mad or not, the Prince of Denmark perished through his confusion about his dead father's will. But our Prince of Peace was never confused. He had the clearest vision of his living Father's will and brought it to a marvellous fulfilment by his perfect resurrection from the dead.

26

Happy the Sinner

In the kingdom that Jesus came to preach there is no room for saints. Only sinners. So if you are a saint already, don't read any further. However if you are conscious of sin in your life, then 'Welcome home!' says the gospel, 'the doors are open to you'. You're in!

Jesus himself was the one who said it. 'I did not come to call the virtuous to repentance,' he announced, 'but sinners' (Lk 5:32). Repentance is the passport to God's kingdom because it is proof of conversion which is the starting point of real holiness.

To illustrate, Christ left us the most plain-speaking of all his parables – about the Pharisee and the tax collector. These men both went into the temple to pray (Lk 18:9-14). The Pharisee marched up to the front and gave thanks that he was so different from the tax collector. 'Everyone knows what they are,' he told God. 'Sharp-shooters! Extortionists! Greedy, dishonest, adulterous and sly!'

Not like the Pharisees, this one in particular. He fasted twice a week, paid his dues, set the right example. 'But,' observed Jesus, 'he was praying to himself'. God wasn't listening. His gaze was fixed on the man at the back, head bowed, humble, confessing his sins. 'I tell you,' finished Jesus, 'this man went back home again justified, at peace with God. The other did not'.

The funny thing is that what the Pharisee said was true. He *was* upright in the moral sense, but his sin was greater than the sins he condemned because he set himself above the mercy of God. He did not need that mercy so he flung it aside, trampled it underfoot even as he stood in God's presence. He failed to realize that there is no salvation without forgiveness and, since only sin merits forgiveness, that there is no salvation without sin.

The tax collector understood this. Which is why he was able to enter the Father's house with confidence, trespasses and all. He was not afraid to face the truth because the truth is that God loves sinners.

Luke's Gospel is very strong on this. He recounts an incident where the parable actually came to life. A prostitute came in and knelt at Jesus' feet when he was dining at the home of a Pharisee named Simon (chapter 7). With her tears she washed the Lord's feet and then dried them with her hair. Like the tax collector, she impressed Jesus deeply with her humility.

Simon the Pharisee however was not at all impressed. How dare this vile woman enter his house and make a fuss? If Jesus were as holy as people made him out to be, surely he would know who it was that touched him! Once again, a Pharisee and a sinner in God's presence. One sorrowful and sincere, the other proud and aloof!

This time, however, the sinner *heard* God's response to the situation. 'The one who has been for given more, loves more,' Christ explained gently to his host. 'This woman has shown much love. Therefore (turning towards her) your sins are pardoned. Go in peace.'

Simon was left speechless, the sadder person. He was incapable of real love. He did not know what it was to be in need of God. And his behaviour bore this out. He had failed to show even the commonest signs of affection for Jesus, the simplest courtesies of a host to a guest. His religion had no warmth in it, no humanity. It was as cold as his heart.

What both stories are telling us is this: that all of us depend on God's mercy for salvation. Even if we are not guilty of grave sin, it is divine mercy that keeps us in grace. When we acknowledge this we become saints. Take for instance the Virgin Mary who was conceived without sin and did nothing displeasing to God. In her great hymn of praise and thanks she rendered back to God the honour he had paid her by preserving her from fault.

My soul rejoices in God my saviour;
He has done great things for me.
He has looked on the lowliness of his handmaid;
And his mercy is from age to age
On those who fear him.

Luke 1:46-55

St Thérèse of Lisieux said the same. God shows his greatest mercy, she wrote, in giving us the grace not to sin.

In other words no matter how blameless we may be, none of us can claim to have remained so without the Father's tender pity towards us. And that is why the Pharisee will always be a stranger in Paradise. The self-righteous simply do not know how to find their way around heaven. The tax collector and the prostitute, Our Lady and St Thérèse all are models of humility. They draw heaven to themselves because they draw the Fatherliness of him who responds only to need.

It was the needy that Jesus drew into his heart on the Cross when he bowed his head before God and prayed for forgiveness. On Calvary his parable achieved the ultimate expression of its truth. For there he so touched the heart of his Father with his own humility that henceforth he unlocked the gates of the kingdom for all who make his prayer for forgiveness their own.

27

The Homecoming

esus' boldest parable, the most stunning of all of them, was his story of the Prodigal Son. Here he set out to do the impossible – to measure the immeasurable mercy of God. It is also the simplest of stories, the most credible. A parent worried about his adolescent child. A son gone off the rails. The generation gap, youthful arrogance, a break from home, a youngster away on his own and no word from him.

Incredibly modern, isn't it? It could be inner-city Glasgow or rural Donegal. The problem of wayward children and heart-broken parents doesn't change very much through the centuries. What makes Jesus' parable so poignant (he understood the pain people go through so well) is the utter goodness of the father of the boy. He didn't cause a row, have a confrontation, utter rash words, bang doors. He just quietly accepted the situation and said nothing as the boy gathered his things – including his father's money – and left.

The man's silence was not indifference. The fact that he ran out to meet his son when the lad returned meant he had been watching out for him at the door. Not just for a day or a week or a month, but for the length of time it takes to squander an inheritance, live a life of debauchery, run out of cash, look for a job, start to feel wretched and decide to come home.

In this the Prodigal's father is like Jesus' Father. Ready to wait a life-time for his children to come to their senses and come back.

And that is what all Jesus' parables are about. A Father

waiting to welcome all who return to him freely, a tender-eyed parent who watches in hope that some day the money will run out and the children will reappear, if for no other reason than that they are hungry and destitute.

It did not matter to the father in the story that his son's return was as selfish as his departure. The boy was shrewd. He sized up his chances when his fortune changed, took advantage of his father's soft-heartedness, and grasped the opportunity of a reconciliation that suited his needs.

A lesser father would have made him work for his keep, repay what he flittered away. But not this one. Because he was like God he threw a party to celebrate his son's coming home. 'He was lost and is found,' he said joyfully, 'was dead and has come back to life'.

So he killed the fatted calf to make it a feast to remember. It was a bit like defrosting the Christmas turkey in October! 'You never did that for me,' complained the other son who was quite unlike his brother. And indeed one can understand his point. It was one thing to take the Prodigal in without recrimination. But to go over the top by slaughtering the calf they had been saving! It was a desperate extravagance. Away beyond what the occasion called for. And totally undeserved. There was no need to humour the brat. Anyone would think that he was being rewarded for his sins.

Why did Jesus have to exaggerate? The story was going really well up to now. Suddenly it had become ridiculous. People would get the wrong impression about God. People would get the wrong idea about sin.

No they wouldn't. Jesus wasn't exaggerating because the reality is even greater than the parable. To celebrate the sinner's conversion it was no fatted calf that God had but his own Beloved Son.

For it is the body of Christ, clubbed and slaughtered on the cross, that provides the food at the reconciliatory meal when wayward sons and daughters come home to him again. The extravagance of God's love beggars the imagination. It doesn't make sense; love never does. No sacrifice is too much when one loves as God loves. One doesn't think when the heart overrides the head. The heavenly Father's heart overrode his head on Good Friday. Jesus saw it coming and accepted it without a murmur. The fact that he composed the parable shows he understood why it had to be done. How else could the world be convinced there is no limit whatever to divine mercy? What better way to persuade the unbelieving?

Isn't it a pity then that so many don't get the message? Or even worse, that they don't care. If they did they would not avoid the home-coming sacrament of reconciliation or absent themselves from the celebratory banquet of the Mass.

28

The Million-Dollar Question

I n looking at Jesus' parables, we notice a pattern emerging. The kingdom of God appears first through conversion of heart, as we turn back again to the Father by listening to Christ. Then through repentance, as we learn to give up sinning and change our sinful ways. Finally, the kingdom blossoms for us under the influence of God's mercy, when we feel his total tenderness towards us in terms of absolute forgiveness.

Our Father's love for us is unconditional; there are no strings attached. We are loved for what we are, not for what we would like to be. Worthiness does not come into it. His love makes us worthy. Being loved by him ennobles us, gives us dignity, makes us holy.

Nevertheless, if the pattern of change and growth is to continue we have to make forgiveness part of our daily mind-set too. If we don't, the beauty in us withers like a rose in December and the fragrance of God's goodness to us disappears. Jesus left us one of his hardest-hitting parables to remind us of this. He put it in the strongest language possible because it is such a vital lesson. Unless you forgive others, you slam the door to forgiveness on yourself.

It is called the *Parable of the Unforgiving Servant* and it was prompted by a question asked of him by Simon Peter the Apostle. 'How often should I forgive my brother if he offends me? As many as seven times?' – the million-dollar question!

In Jesus' day, 'seven' meant 'a lot'. But even a lot comes to an end. Does there come a time, Simon Peter is asking, when it is permissible to stop forgiving? When a person repeatedly annoys you, insults you, even injures you, and you say to yourself, 'Enough is enough. I have run out of absolutions and free pardons'.

Let us suppose, replies Jesus to Peter, that the answer is Yes. Supposing it is all right to withhold forgiveness after a reasonable amount of patience. If it is fair in one case, it is fair in all. That means that God should be allowed the same right. In which case, we are all snookered. For already we have used up our 'seven' chances. Every day we have to ask God's pardon for a million offences, small or great, committed through thoughtlessness, or in passion, or with cool, deliberate intent.

As the *Book of Proverbs* (24:16) says, even 'the virtuous man falls seven times' and is able to get up again only because he is sure of God's love for him. If you take the hope of that love away, none of us would be able to rise even once, and then where would we be? On the other hand, why should God be expected to overlook the repeated offence if we do not expect the same of ourselves when dealing with others?

To make the message really clear, Jesus turned it into a sharp little piece of role-play (Mt 18.23-35). Imagine you are Minister of Finance in the government of an ancient near-Eastern state. You overspend the National Budget by a couple of billion dollars, the markets collapse, you borrow and cannot pay back, you are in the soup up to your neck.

So there is no alternative: it is life imprisonment with hard labour (and because this is two thousand years ago, your wife and children must go to prison too).

What is to be done in such a desperate situation? You might grasp at a straw, like the servant, who 'fell on his knees, imploring his master, *Lord, have patience with me, and I will pay you every thing'*. Some hope! Who could pay back the National Debt from his Post-Office Savings Account! Never in a million years.

His Prime Minister, however, was an unusually understanding man, so 'out of pity for him he forgave him the whole debt and released him'. Just like that! Now he could forget about the crisis; he would be back in his office again on Monday morning after a relaxing weekend at home with his wife and children.

Before he joined the joyful Friday traffic out of the city, he ran into a chap who was a labourer and owed him a few weeks' salary. It would have amounted to about £650, not as much as the National Debt admittedly but more than enough to buy a nice meal with a bottle of wine to celebrate his narrow escape with the Exchequer. 'And seizing him by the throat (his manners were not all they might have been) he said, "Pay me what you owe"', and simply closed his ears to his fellow servant's plea for time.

Well obviously the Sunday tabloids got hold of the story and it was front page gossip in every newsagent's two mornings later. Pictures and all. It reached the breakfast tables in high places too. When the Prime Minister read the details he dropped his knife and fork, reached for the phone and immediately set up an inquiry.

Our friend's quiet weekend was rudely brought to a close. He himself was rudely brought to the Magistrate's court, and the outcome was too terrible to go into further detail on.

Jesus would have paused to let Peter take it in. The Apostle would have glanced up at him and smiled. Jesus always made his point with a bang. How he exaggerated in his stories to enlarge his meaning! How humorous he could be in his portrayal of human nature! And yet what he said was true. Blown up large, magnified, his parable uncovered a simple little truth whose spirit we conveniently overlook when it suits us.

'So, not seven then,' Simon Peter would have echoed, repeating the Master's opening words, 'but seventy times seven'. That's how often we are pardoned by him of a debt against God which is too high for any of us to make good. And to let us go free he would pay the full debt with his blood on Good Friday.

In the circumstances, Peter would have to agree. It is only logical that we too should 'forgive your brother from your heart'. Without conditions. Without strings attached. As often as is required. Just like God himself.

The rose that blooms in December is even more lovely than the one that blossoms in June.

29

How to Wear God Down

esus recommended nagging as a good way to get what you want out of God. If you nag him enough, he suggested, the Father will be glad to give you all you ask before long. For God has a low resistance to any one who harps on and on at him. And Jesus should know for he is his Son.

It is a curious way to think of prayer but it is the way Christ presented it to his disciples. In the parable of the poor widow and the unjust judge, for example (Lk18:1-8). She lived in the same city as he did and would come to his door every day in person to get a legal judgement from him against those who were harassing her. If she had lived today she would probably have phoned him as well, written to his secretary, faxed his office, intruded on his golf.

But because she was not important, he did not give her much attention. He had more lucrative cases on his desk, more prestigious decisions to consider. Had he been a conscientious man, his sense of right and wrong might have persuaded him to help her. But he was not. He didn't believe in God and cared little for what others thought of him.

On the face of it her chances were not good. Who else was there to plead her cause? She didn't know the kind of people who can pull strings.

And yet she had one resource, this crafty pensioner, one asset greater than any other. Determination. Once she got a notion in her head she would not rest until it was resolved. So she made a nuisance of herself.

What had she to lose? She did not mind if he was driven

to the brink of exasperation. All she wanted was her legal rights – and she was determined to get them. So she nagged and harped and called and pleaded and begged and cajoled until he was sick of her.

Finally he could ignore her no more. 'Maybe I neither fear God nor regard man,' he said to himself at last, 'yet because this widow bothers me, I will vindicate her, or she will wear me out by her continual coming.'

'Consider what the unjust judge says,' counselled Jesus; 'Will God not vindicate his elect, who cry to him day and night? Will he delay long over them? I tell you, he will vindicate them speedily'.

The thing about Jesus' parables is they are so logical! So utterly credible. What he says in this instance about intercessory prayer makes sense. If God is truly our Father, how could he refuse his children anything? Even imperfect parents will give in to their demanding offspring if only to get peace.

Jesus indeed made the point once before in Luke's Gospel to a crowd of men who had gathered to listen to his teaching. 'What father among you,' he said to them, 'if his son asks for a fish will give him a serpent; or if he asks for an egg, will give him a scorpion? If you, then, who are evil know how to give good gifts to your children, how much more will the heavenly Father give the Holy Spirit to those who ask him?' (Lk 11.11-13).

He needn't have said any more. He was speaking a language they could understand. They were convinced by an argument that matched their own experience.

But he did say more. 'Ask, and it will be given to you; seek and you will find; knock, and the door will be opened to you.'

Sometimes the message has to be spelled out for us, even though we know it makes eminent sense. And in the story about the nagging widow, 'he told them this parable to show the need to pray continually and never lose heart' – the voice of St Luke chipping in to make sure we got it the first time.

Why do we all need reminding and encouragement in prayer? Because we are easily put off. If our requests are not answered straightaway, we give up; if other people stop praying, so do we; if we don't hear God's voice, we think he doesn't hear ours.

Think again, urges Jesus, and the gospel repeats his advice like an echo down through the ages: think again, think again. Has there ever been anyone who petitioned persistently and walked away empty? Do you imagine for one moment then that you are going to be the first?

30

The Pearl

I f brevity is the soul of story-telling as an art, then Jesus' shortest parable is his best. *The Pearl* is not only the briefest of his compositions but also the most remarkable, as we shall see.

A merchant with an eye to beauty one day finds what he has been seeking for a long time – a pearl rich and lustrous, perfect in shape and flawless. A pearl of pearls, translucent as the warm waters of the Red Sea from which it came. At once he sells everything he has and goes off and buys it. Without so much as a second thought. Though left with nothing but the clothes he stands in, he considers himself the luckiest man in the world. A once-in-a-lifetime chance presented itself and he took it. 'And that,' said Jesus, 'is precisely what the Kingdom of heaven is like' (Mt 13.45).

I wonder how the merchant's wife reacted when he got home – if he still had a home to go to, that is. Presumably that too was sold to raise the money.

Can you imagine her face? Not a loaf of bread in the kitchen, but this magnificent pearl in the parlour that nobody wanted! Not a shilling in the coffers but a priceless jewel on their hands that was good for nothing! I would love to have heard him trying to justify himself!

Wasn't Jesus odd to tell such a ridiculous story. Surely he did not approve of the merchant's madness. To squander all your resources on an obsession? Even if precious stones were his trade, you don't risk your all on a single pearl.

But then Jesus wasn't talking about pearls. What he had in mind was something much more magnificent. The kingdom of heaven. A new relationship with God. Life in the Holy Spirit. The gospel. Here was a treasure worth the investment.

Falling in love with God turns everything into an adventure. It makes problems irrelevant. It changes the way things look. It alters the way you feel. As with any love-affair it brings a new purpose to all that is ordinary.

Even the simple things you do take on an eternal significance. Other people become easier to handle. Once-difficult tasks become effortless. Your attitude to yourself blossoms. Negative self-criticism disappears. Guilt, fear, insecurity evaporate. You are conscious only of a quiet dignity, of your worthiness of love.

How was Jesus to put such an ideal existence across? By what means might he convey the effect God's love has on us when we allow ourselves to be captivated by it? How might he persuade us that such a gift is within everyone's reach if only we stopped to look?

Then one day as Jesus wandered alone through the crowded market-squares and bazaars of Jerusalem at festival time, he saw some merchants of fine pearls displaying their wares. He watched the enthusiasm with which men respond to sheer beauty. Their recklessness as they barter to buy. Their efforts to meet the price, their pledges of assets as payment in kind.

And as he looked on, Jesus would have understood their obsession. For people are fascinated by beauty. It allures them, enchants them, makes them oblivious to reason. If pearls can do this, he must have thought, how much more the treasure I bring!

The scene would have stayed in his mind. Later he was to tell his disciples, as they set off to preach the gospel, 'Do not cast your pearls before swine' (Mt 7:6), meaning, 'The Good News is too precious to waste where it is not valued'. And later still the very gates of heaven would be described as carved each from a single pearl! (Rev 21:21).

An image had been found to portray the splendour of God, the delight of his dwelling-place, the richness of his love. Part of their attraction was their newness. Pearls are never mentioned in the Old Testament for the simple reason they were not discovered until about 300 BC. They belong to the New Testament, and like the Good News it proclaims, they were quite different from any of the precious stones known before. Just as Jesus himself was quite different from the prophets or Moses or Abraham. Like the oysters that held their radiant secret for centuries until now, so the heavenly Father was at last disclosing the translucence of his kingdom through the teaching and works of the Son.

'At that same hour Jesus rejoiced in the Holy Spirit and said, "I thank you, Father, Lord of heaven and earth, because you have hidden these things from the learned and the clever and have revealed them to mere children"; then turning to his disciples, he said to them privately, "Blessed are the eyes that see what you see! For I tell you that many prophets and kings desired to see what you see, but did not see it, and to hear what you hear, but did not hear it"' (Lk 10:21; 23-24).

In the world of Christian standards the merchant of the parable is the one who has heard the call to love in Jesus' voice, and been stunned; who has perceived the way Jesus gently changes people's lives, and been deeply moved; who has recognized the irresistible quality of Christ's character, and been enthralled by the Person of Jesus himself.

The merchant today therefore is any man or woman who, attracted by the beauty of God's Son, cannot help but respond with a love in kind that is freely returned and is generous and full.

31

Rachel

Rachel is an Old Testament character who is remembered in the opening pages of the New Testament. In Matthew's Christmas story she is portrayed 'weeping for her children', refusing to be consoled. The scene is the massacre of the innocents. In a mad attempt to eliminate the new-born Jesus, Herod has all the male children under two years old murdered in the Bethlehem area. Obsessed with getting the right child, he simply slaughters all the children in a paroxysm of cruelty unparalleled since the destruction of the Hebrew infants under Pharaoh at the time of Moses' birth.

Rachel – who herself died giving birth – was buried just outside Bethlehem at Ramah more than a thousand years before. It was almost as if, Matthew seems to be saying, her voice could be heard sobbing from the grave as the blood of the innocents washed over her tomb:

> *A voice was heard at Ramah,*
> *wailing and loud lamentation,*
> *Rachel weeping for her children;*
> *she refused to be consoled,*
> *because they were no more.*
> Matthew 2:18

She is the symbol of a nation's grief. Wife of Jacob, father of the twelve tribes, she is Mother Israel, a tragic figure of suffering at the deepest level. Her lament lingers down the long centuries of her country's misfortunes, bewailing the wilful extermination of her offspring in every age.

Six centuries before Christ, for instance, in the prophet Jeremiah's time, Ramah was the mournful site of a Jewish concentration camp where all able-bodied Israelites were rounded up by the Babylonians to be force-marched off into exile. Roped together one to another like slaves, they were herded across the desert on a bitter six-week trek to a foreign land, their eyes dim with tears as they looked back at the smoke rising from their beloved country now in ruins. To the prophet it seemed as they passed where Rachel's hallowed bones were laid to rest, the Mother of the Nation herself was weeping uncontrollably with them in their defeat.

Throughout the history of the Chosen People Rachel must never have stopped crying. There was always so much to shed tears for. The suffering of the guiltless, violence and bloodshed, crime and destruction, exile and defeat. And always it was the poor of the nation who endured the most. Women and children, mothers, widows, orphans, who had no power or influence to change the way things were. Victims, all of them, of forces greater than themselves: the psychopathic jealousy of kings, the insecurity and fear of governments, the compulsive blood-lust of war lords.

Rachel's motherly grieving is like the grieving of God himself. Silently mourning his people's plight. Moved with compassion for their hardship at each stage of their story. Sharing all that his beloved children had to go through, feeling what they felt, understanding their hopes, their despair.

When Christ was born, God entered into human pain. The divine mystery intersected human history, forming the cross. It was God's most convincing act of solidarity. He could have remained apart, absented himself from their lot, but he didn't. He could have taken pain away altogether, but he didn't do that either. Through his new-born child he took humanity into his arms, took Rachel's grief upon himself and made it his own. In this way he transformed the agony people go through – not just that of the Jews, but everyone's – and gave it new meaning, endowing pain with the power to redeem.

Rachel's ghostly appearance at the start of the gospel is a sober reminder that Christ was born to die. Her tearful presence makes us think of the kind of world he came into – ruthless and violent and Godless. She is an omen of dark things to come, of the terrible opposition that was to shadow Jesus from the start of his life to the end, of the pitiless suffering he would one day have to confront himself. The bloodshed that marked his birth would also mark his death. He would take it upon himself voluntarily for the sake of the kingdom of heaven, in order to dry Rachel's tears and remove the mourning veil from her children's faces. To give hope again where there was only despair. To put new heart into the helpless by becoming a helpless child himself.

This is why the Church celebrates martyrdom immediately after Christmas. First the birth of the Saviour, then the stoning of Stephen (December 26th). First the joy of Nativity, then the death of the innocents (December 28th). First the celebration of life, then the stabbing of Thomas à Becket in his cathedral at Canterbury (December 29th). Before Christmas week is out, three major feasts of martyrs. And yet these are celebrations of victory, not dirges of defeat. For the Church knows that when the cross is read back into the Christmas story Rachel's prayer to God is answered. Her children do not die in vain, for they die in Christ as all must die in Christ who wish to live the new life that his birth makes possible.

32

What Jesus Saw

A mong the handful of people in the gospel that Jesus really admired and marked out as worthy of imitation, the most surprising was the poor widow who put all of two small coins into the temple treasury (Mk 12:41-44).

It is amazing that he even noticed her. There were more interesting people in the crowd that day as it milled in and out of the temple precincts. Yet as Jesus sat and watched them, it was none of these that moved him. Not the sleek and well-dressed, nor the young and energetic, nor the pick-pockets and hangers-on. It was the elderly pensioner alone.

She wasn't rich, she didn't have poise or appearance, she didn't have social graces. But she did have generosity. Jesus turned to his disciples and nodded toward the old Biddy. 'Truly, I say to you,' he announced, 'this poor widow has put in more than all those who are contributing to the treasury. For they all contributed out of their abundance; but she out of her poverty has put in everything she had, her whole living'.

Her contribution that day amounted to the grand total of one penny. Hardly enough to buy oil for the lamp in the doorway! But it was all she had, it constituted her entire income. So in donating her penny she had in fact sacrificed herself. And to Jesus, the gift of self counts for more than anything else in the world.

There are three reasons why he singled her out for attention. First, she was a photo-copy of Jesus himself. 'Though he was rich', says St Paul of Christ, 'yet for your sake he became poor, so that by his poverty you might become rich' (2 Cor 8:9). In God's hands, poverty is power. The less there is to come and go on, the more he can do. This is because it is love that changes people, not material resources. And when love is given freely and fully, it renews the face of the earth. So when divine love appeared in the flesh in the Person of Jesus, God purposely laid aside as much of the glory and the grandeur as he could to let that love be seen in all its naked tenderness and simplicity, to show how powerfully it can transform lives. And then, like the widow at the treasury, he poured it all out on saint and sinner alike, completely.

On the surface – again like the poor widow – Jesus did not have much to offer the world. No food and agriculture programmes, no economic reforms, no hospitals or schools (and yet all of these would come through men and women committed to the values of the gospel). What he did bring to enrich the world was a new dignity for human nature, a new self respect, inner peace through reconciliation with the Father in heaven. To achieve this, he accepted the ultimate poverty of the cross. Left stripped and wounded in a thousand places, he held back nothing for himself, not even his life. To the Greek and Roman mind he looked like a simpleton, so insignificant they barely noticed him at all; there were after all so many other interesting people to look at in Jerusalem at that time. But to those who take note of generosity, who do appreciate what it is to give one's all, here was a model that inspired, a force to dislocate the power of hell.

The second reason Jesus drew attention to the widow was she exemplified what he wanted his Church to be: a generous presence in the world that would make his own self-giving available to everyone. The Church was to be his body; he would be its head. What he had done in his lifetime must not end when he returned to the Father. He would still have hands on earth to bless and heal, feet to visit the sick and imprisoned, eyes to see human need, ears to listen with compassion, a voice to console and forgive and to challenge. They would be the members of his churchly body. Through them he would extend his personal love to the end of time.

To be true to his Spirit, the Church would therefore do his work best when it was poorest. For then the power of its ministry would clearly be seen as his power, not anyone else's. And that is the way it has always been. When the Church is at its weakest the grace it channels has always been strongest. When it has been stripped of influence, prestige and popularity, and yet continued to preach the gospel and celebrate the sacraments with faith in God and charity towards the world, the Christian community has always been most what he wanted it to be. For it is through the fidelity and endurance of those who work to serve God and others and not themselves, that the triumph of the cross once again touches hearts, converts, saves.

Thirdly, Jesus saw in the old widow a pattern for individual happiness and fulfilment. 'God loves a cheerful giver,' wrote St Paul (2 Cor 9:7). In other words, people who are generous are joyful in themselves. They have learned to go beyond their own needs, to think about others instead, to find satisfaction in contributing. They have escaped from the sad prison of their ego. To meet them is to know Christ and experience his goodness. One immediately feels at ease with such a person, unthreatened, affirmed.

I remember an elderly nun telling how she passed a group of disadvantaged children in an inner city parish where she worked. One cheeky cub sat dangling his feet, watching her curiously as she went by. 'Hey, Missus!' he shouted suddenly, 'What did Jesus ever see in you?'

'And were you annoyed?' someone asked her later. 'No,' she replied with a good natured chuckle; 'I've often asked myself the same question!'

What did Jesus see in you, I thought to myself as I listened. Why, he saw in her what he once saw in the poor widow at the temple treasury!

33

The Zeal of Mrs Zebedee

Mrs Zebedee in the gospel had, as you might say, some neck. When you read what she did to advance the prospects of her two sons, James and John, it makes you whistle appreciatively at her audacity. It also makes you realise that some mothers don't change no matter how far back you go: the pushy ones, the grossly ambitious.

She was cute in the way she did it: came straight up to Jesus with the boys on either side and 'kneeling before him asked him for something' (Mt 20:20). How could he resist! All the right moves to absorb his attention: the proper demeanour, the humble approach, the anxious mother bit, the pleading eyes. No wonder the other apostles watched her curiously, suspiciously.

She was not the type to miss an opportunity, this one. She could see that Jesus was not your ordinary young rabbi – they all could. He had a future before him. He would go places. Already he was modestly famous and very popular. All those healings of his, his magnetic words, the way he drew people after him – the shady dealers, the disreputable, the outcasts. How they melted under his influence, turned over a new leaf, became somebodies!

Everyone she talked to agreed that he was the Messiah, the promised Deliverer foretold by the prophets, the one through whom God would establish the kingdom in Israel again. While no one was quite sure what that meant precisely, Mrs Zebedee had her own whimsical idea. It could only mean power and glory, and plenty of it.

What a stroke of good fortune just begging to be tapped!

Not for herself, of course, but for her Jimmy and her Johnny. Handled shrewdly, here was the chance for them to make a name for themselves, be more than poor fishermen who worked late shifts and got very little in return for their efforts at sea.

It was not as if her boys were on the fringe. They were already part of Jesus' inner circle, his close associates. But they were two among twelve, and not everybody can come double-first. A little push from mother might just swing the balance in their favour. And why not? Jesus was so responsive to people who knelt before him. If she didn't, someone else would; someone always did. You have to be pretty quick in life to put your spoke in, or you will be pushed aside before you can say, Thy Kingdom come!

So Jesus said to her, 'What do you want?' She said to him, 'Command that these two sons of mine may sit, one at your right hand and one at your left, in your kingdom.'

The gospel doesn't say that Jesus actually laughed. He never laughed at anyone's prayer on their knees. But he stifled some reaction to such a misplaced petition. The poor woman obviously didn't understand anything about his mission on earth: his vocation to suffering, his commitment to the cross. The kingdom he had in mind was no worldly affair. It was to be a reign of love through pain, not an empire. This king would be his people's servant, not their dictator. The crown he would wear would be of thorns, not gold. His throne would be a gibbet, not a seat of splendour. He would conquer his enemies by making them friends, not by condemning them. There would be no glory in this, not the kind she expected. No triumphal processions, no tributes from vassals, no titles of renown. Just blood and sweat and tears, hardship, and self-sacrifice in the service of others.

'You do not know what you are asking,' Jesus said to her kindly, and then to James and John, 'Are you able to drink the cup that I am to drink?' It was the cup of bitterness and anguish, the same chalice Jesus himself had to pray to be able to accept in the Garden of Gethsemane. It would have to be drained to the dregs before the Father's will could be accomplished.

It was the very cup Jesus offered his disciples at the Last Supper on the eve of his passion. 'This is the cup of my blood,' he told them. Whoever shared this drink would be expected to share all that it symbolised: the pouring out of one's life for sinners, the total giving of oneself for those in need. Participation in the Eucharist would always mean participation in Christ's death. There would be no room at this meal for selfish ambition, jealousy, domination, disharmony or self-righteousness.

By now the other apostles had got Mrs Zebedee's full drift. Suddenly they were outraged. How dare this woman and her sons try to get one over them! How dare they try to step out in front of everyone to be first! In the fracas that followed, Jesus sighed. So he called them to him and said, 'Whoever would be great among you must be your servant, and whoever would be first among you must be your slave; even as the Son of man came not to be served but to serve, and to give his life as a ransom for many'.

If that didn't sober them up, Good Friday did. For there Jesus turned his words into a shape they were not to forget. Not only in his living did he show the depth of his commitment to people; in his dying he demonstrated how seriously he meant what he said.

If all the disciples were given something to think about that day on the road when they nearly came to blows, it was Mrs Zebedee who took the lesson soonest to heart. The next time we hear of her in the gospel is at Calvary. She was one of the very few, according to Matthew, who followed Jesus along the way of the cross and stayed with him while he died. Her attitude had changed. Gone were the foolish fantasies. How quickly this mother grasped the mind of Christ and rearranged her view of what was important and what was not.

Maybe that's why she and her sons are still remembered and greatly honoured on earth and in heaven today.

34

Women at Calvary

There were two groups of women with Jesus at Calvary as he died on the cross. One was the Daughters of Jerusalem; the other, those who followed him during his ministry in Galilee. All of them comforted him in the most dreadful moments of his passion and stood by him until he breathed his last. Their loyalty was remarkable in that they did this on their own, for nearly all Jesus' male disciples fled at the first sign of trouble.

The Daughters of Jerusalem were a charitable company of matrons who offered assistance to criminals on their way to execution. They would take with them a mixture of wine and myrrh as a painkiller to ease the agony of dying. They did not care who the criminal was. They saw only a human being in pain, and had pity. Their very great charity was rewarded one day when the criminal they assisted was Jesus.

The second group, from Galilee, were no strangers to him. They travelled round the towns and villages of his early days with him as he preached and healed and taught. They not only listened to his words and experienced his grace; they also provided out of their own means whatever was needed for his nourishment and welfare. Now they could do no more than stay when all others deserted him.

Women were always the most faithful to Christ in the gospels. This is why they held a special place in his affection. They seemed to draw out of him all his gentleness and humanity. There was something in the feminine character that he responded to with particular tenderness. Maybe it was because as man he knew the image of God in humankind is perfected in both the male and the female together. *The Book of Genesis* after all depicted God imprinting His likeness on people as men and as women – 'So God created man in his own image, in the image of God he created him; male and female he created them' (1:27).

Knowing this, Jesus looked to his female disciples to help him complete the image of God in his own life on earth. They embodied the Church as Christ's helpmate – a new Eve for a new Adam – in extending God's creative dominion over the new creation. Since he was to achieve this by the outpouring of compassion on all humanity, they would play an indispensable role in his plan. For women are naturally compassionate; it is part of the feminine character. While men are not incapable of kindness and pity, they are less sensitive by nature. Women know how to feel deeply by instinct; it is part of their strength as women. This is why they understand the mind of Christ so readily, reflect his tender-heartedness so easily.

In Jesus' eyes they represent his Church as wife and mother. From the very beginning of his ministry he drew them after him. He wanted them to learn from his divine gentleness to recognize the same in themselves: his patience with people; his understanding of children; his concern for the sick; his quickness to forgive when let down; his loyalty in friendship; his dependability in self-giving. It was on the cross that these qualities were revealed in their fullness. So it is no surprise that women were present at the cross. This was the apex of their apprenticeship in compassion. Jesus specifically desired them to be with him there. His grace enabled them to complete the journey, to finish the course.

When he saw them weeping helplessly for him, it lifted his heart. They were like himself – caught in a spiral of violence though innocent of crime, torn apart emotionally through their involvement in love. Though racked with pain in his body and soul, his heart went out to them in their distress.

'Do not weep for me', he offered consolingly, 'but weep

for yourselves and for your children'. He could see what still lay ahead of them. Jerusalem would be destroyed by the Romans in a matter of years. They and their descendants would be mercilessly slaughtered. Women have always been the Christs of history, victims of sin that is not their own, causalities left to pick up the pieces, sufferers expected to heal the suffering.

Jesus sanctified their sufferings from the cross. From his opened side he poured out the blood and water of his life upon the ground where they stood. As he bowed his head in death he breathed his spirit upon them with his last breath. Even as they watched, these women witnessed the birth of the Church. This water, this spirit prefigured the baptism by which many would be reborn. This blood symbolised the Eucharist by which many would be nourished and grow strong. It was as if Jesus, like a mother dying in child-birth, was showing them through his labour how to give life and sustain life with love. Such would be the vocation of his Church.

When it was fully assembled, the women would tell what they saw; would explain to the men the meaning of pain; together with them would support and encourage the early faith community in its infancy; would remind the new converts of the source of their hope. And from that witness would arise the tradition of grace and fellowship, care and compassion we call Christianity.

The witnesses at Calvary were also, significantly, first to experience the resurrection. Having stood by Jesus in his dying, they continued to stand by his tomb where they returned after the Sabbath. They were singularly rewarded on Easter morning when he revealed to them – before anyone else – his risen glory. Then he sent them as apostles to the Apostles to proclaim the Paschal creed that Life had triumphed over death, Love over hatred. Their privileged commission is a lasting reminder that whoever remains faithful to Christ in his passion will be given the secret of joy – even if they are men!

35

The Widow of Nain

The Jews of Jesus' time always buried their dead outside the walls of their town or village. Death had to be kept at a distance. A corpse was an unclean thing, it was not welcome in the community of the living. The deceased had their own place, the necropolis or city of the dead, located in the surrounding hills. There the remains were laid in one of the caves, its entrance sealed with a gigantic boulder forever.

The road to the necropolis was a road of sorrow. Along this path Jesus walked one day on his way to the city of Nain with his disciples and a large crowd of followers. Suddenly from the city gate emerged a huge cortege of mourners carrying out the body of a man who had just died. It was a very sad affair. He had been a young man, about Jesus' age. His fellow townsmen and friends were openly distressed. But saddest of all was his mother who had to be supported for grief as she walked beside his remains.

Jesus was immediately moved with pity. 'Do not weep,' he said to the woman as the procession approached, and he stopped the funeral bier with his hand.

There were several reasons for Jesus' compassion. Funerals always upset him. He could not bear it when people died. He hated to see relatives in distress. He hated mourning and bereavements and tears and grief. Here was a whole town in mourning. This was someone's mother in tears. Extremely sensitive to people in pain, his heart was easily touched by such a scene.

But there was another reason too. This woman was a widow. The dead man was her only son. She would have no one to provide for her now. There was no social security to see her through, no state benefits, no widow's pension. No anything. What was she going to do? Jewish society did not concern itself about women who lived alone. They had to shift for themselves as best they could. Such poor widows often had no option but to go begging simply to eat. So in addition to the agonizing loss of a loved one was the worrying loss of her livelihood. Jesus grasped the implications of her predicament in an instant. He understood exactly how she felt.

But the main reason for his pity was more significant than these. As he watched this woman lamenting her son he saw another mother mourning. She was a widow too, the dead man also an only son. Like the widow of Nain she had no one to support her either, none to share her solitude.

He could see her lean over the lifeless form of her beloved child, his body not yet cold, his bearded face aghast in death, his limbs limp and bloodless, the raw flesh torn and exposed above his heart. He watched the stunned grief on the Virgin's face as they laid her son in her lap, her eyes heavy with pain, their light extinguished. Then the wrapping of the corpse in a shroud, the winding of the napkin round the head, the hurried procession to the tomb. He saw his mother, steadied by kindly hands, follow close beside his remains.

Jesus would not be able to help her. He would have to rely on others to see her through. John, the Beloved Disciple. Joseph of Arimathea. Mary of Magdala. To anyone who could help he would be grateful.

'Do not weep,' he found himself saying as he came back to the present, his hand on the bier as the bearers stood still. And turning to the corpse 'he said, "Young man, I say to you arise". And the dead man sat up, and began to speak. And Jesus gave him to his mother' (Lk 7:14-15).

Death would not have the last word, for love is stronger than death. Love breaks out of tombs, removes gigantic boulders. Because love lasts forever, many waters cannot quench it, no torrent can destroy it. Not even the course of nature can extinguish it, for love is supernatural. All things come to an end except love, for love is of God. As long as there is a God in heaven, as long as there is a God on earth, death is only a resting place where love returns to God in whom it is perfected. And when it is perfected it will unite once more all those who claim love as their own, but in a unity so strong that the former pain of parting will be forgotten. For then it will be purified of the selfishness which alone wrecks relationships by putting love aside.

By his raising of the dead, by his own resurrection, Jesus gave his words 'Do not weep' a force. Without denying the human process of bereavement, so necessary for accepting reality, he unveiled the fullness of reality: that those who live and die for others now will find they have lost nothing in the kingdom where funerals are unknown and necropolis is a meaningless term.

Anyone who knows Jesus, knows that.

36

Apostle of the Ascension

veryone knows that Mary Magdalene was the first witness of the Resurrection. What is not so well remembered is that she was first to proclaim the Ascension too. First *apostle* of the Ascension in fact. 'Apostle' means one who is sent, specially commissioned. 'Go to my brothers,' Jesus instructed her, 'and say to them, "I am ascending to my Father and your Father, to my God and your God"' (Jn 20:17). Which she did: 'Mary Magdalene went and said to the disciples, "I have seen the Lord"; and she told them that he had said all these things to her' (Jn 20:18).

The disciples were understandably sceptical because of who she was. She was a woman first of all, and in Jewish society women did not have any standing as witnesses, did not have a voice. But more: this was a person from whom Jesus had cast out *no fewer than seven devils*. Some people think she may have been the prostitute Jesus defended from public condemnation, thus saving her from stoning and restoring her self-respect. Possibly she was the harlot who washed his feet with her tears and dried them with her hair. Tradition tends to identify her with all of these, and religious art usually depicts her in hues of red and purple kneeling contrite at the foot of the cross.

What is certain is a) that she was a remarkable convert to Christ, and b) that she occupied a position of enormous importance in the early Church because of her proclamation of the Easter message. Indeed she is mentioned more often in the New Testament than any other woman except the Virgin Mary.

The reason Jesus told her about his Ascension was to stop her clinging to his feet. 'Do not hold on to me', he said to her gently, 'for I have not yet ascended to the Father'. She could not help it; she was so unspeakably moved at seeing him again after.

Here was the only man who ever understood her. No other person touched her heart with such compassion, such tenderness. In his presence she found her dignity again, learned to love herself as a woman of worth. Not an object to be used by others, then thrown aside, but a human being in whom the image of God was shaped, earning her the right to decency and respect. Then he had died and she had lost him, lost herself as well. Now he was standing before her very eyes, incredible though that was, and for fear of losing him a second time she threw her arms around him tightly so that he could barely move. Such was the reality of the Resurrection to Mary of Magdala!

But, 'Do not hold on to me', he was saying, 'I have not yet ascended'. What on earth did he mean? Was he about to leave her again? Did he no longer wish to know her? Did he wish to distance himself from them all because they had denied him? She did not understand the Ascension and probably did not want to.

Jesus in fact meant none of these things. By returning to the Father he intended giving himself to her more completely than in any physical embrace. He would do so by sending his Spirit. And not only to Mary Magdalene but to all his disciples. That Spirit would make him present not simply to the eye, but to the very heart and soul of those who believed in him. He would dwell in each and all together in the community we call the Church.

His personality would be felt as grace. His mind, alive in their thoughts, would move them to holy intentions and empower them to carry these out. His generous forgiveness would so console and reassure them, they would begin to live the Resurrection themselves by forgiving others in turn. And especially through the Eucharist they would become with him one flesh as a bride becomes one with her husband.

But first he must return to the Father to bring all humanity to heaven in his own humanity. Breaking through the dark barriers of death, like the morning sun climbing to its noon-day height, he would pour down from his Father's house the brilliant radiance of the Father's love upon all who live in the light. Excluding none, as daylight excludes none, he would fill the earth with his fullest self in a way that would last forever. Thereafter no one would need to search for him by going a distance or waiting for the life to come. They would find him no further away than in themselves and in those they love.

And that is why Mary Magdalene had to let him go, as we all have to let others go if we wish to keep them close. Real love means that we don't try to possess another by clinging. So good parents let their children grow and leave home; wise children yield their parents to death and to God; mature spouses permit each other space for personal development; true friends allow each other other friendships, and so on.

This was the message the Magdalene was sent to announce. That healthy intimacy (in its various forms) is always spiritual, has a divine dimension, is holy. Because this is so it cannot abide possessiveness or the dominance of one over another. Such things only lead to crucifixion and sealing people up in closed tombs.

That wasn't the type of intimacy Jesus wanted with anyone. It was not in his nature to smother and he didn't want to be smothered himself. The closeness he had to offer was the kind that sets others free to be faithful since love is not love until it is given without compulsion.

The Jews of his time did not see it that way. They wanted to have Christ on their terms, make him conform, tone him down, bring him under control, and when they couldn't they tied him up and pinned him fast and buried him under the ground.

But true intimacy, like Jesus himself, rises above what is earthly. It knows how to ascend to a different level altogether where human beings relate to each other in such a way that they can also relate to God.

That Jesus chose a former prostitute to proclaim his Ascension is significant. It means that even those who have been maltreated or abused can become apostles. They are not doomed to be perpetually suspicious of friends who truly love them. Through one's closeness to Christ it is possible to learn to trust again, to ascend with him 'to his Father and their Father', to channel his love in a human way by sharing his life-giving Spirit.

Mary Magdalene is proof, as the Risen Jesus himself is proof, that Ascension is open to all.

37

Poverty of Spirit

The story the Gospel tells us is not just Jesus' story. It is ours too, narrated in the quality of our lives as Christians. Whoever follows Jesus reproduces his personal characteristics, extends them into the everyday situations that go to make up the gospel of living. Where these qualities appear they are signs that the kingdom Jesus preached is in our midst. Just as he embodied God's kingdom in his life on earth – in his attitudes, his outlook, his perceptions, his decisions – so those who live as he lived, embody him.

We call these qualities the Beatitudes – eight statements of blessedness that together make up a kind of identikit picture of Jesus himself. Wherever they are found, there Christ's portrait is photocopied in the features of his followers. The blessed are those who have achieved – or received – an inner tranquillity that is enviable. It comes to them through their exposure to the word of God in all its many dimensions as Good News.

First among these beatitudes is poverty of spirit. 'Blessed are the poor in spirit', Jesus taught, 'for theirs is the kingdom of heaven' (Mt 5:3).

You can recognize the poor in spirit easily. They are approachable, understanding and helpful. They are also people who carry a cross. As you get to know them you will find that the two aspects are linked: they understand you because they are human themselves; they are compassionate because they know what it is to suffer. That is why they will never try to dominate you, or patronize you or put you down. They would feel they had no right.

You will also find they are optimistic in outlook. Not in the sense of *David Copperfield's* Mr Micawber, the ne'er-do-well who waited around idly for 'something to turn up'. But in the sense that something good does turn up when you do everything you can to make it.

The poor in spirit therefore are early risers, hard workers and persistent triers. Not even their crosses prevent them from looking for the bright side. Indeed they search for it all the more when it is harder to find.

We are not just talking here about personality types. The truly poor cut across all natures. So what is the secret that makes them stand out as attractive human beings, the sort that draw admiration? It is their utter dependence on God. Because the cross they carry is a heavy one, they have to trust him alone. Day by day they turn to the Father in their poverty of heart, believing he will see them through, that he will help them to cope. And day by day they find their hope is not in vain.

Their cross may be a recent bereavement, a terrible sense of loneliness, a drink problem; sometimes it is an unhappy marriage, wayward children, severe depression, or just simply 'nerves'.

Experience teaches them that these things can actually make you a better person – more patient for example, more humble. And so, relying on a strength greater than their own, they redouble their efforts to do the best they can.

The truth is that all of us are impoverished without God. When we recognize this we inherit the kingdom of heaven. When we deny it we inherit merely the passing kingdoms of the modern world. The kingdom of heaven brings inner peace and strength. The others bring frustration and unhappiness. When we try to go it alone, using only our own resources, we fail. When we make use of the helps that God offers, we succeed.

It is not that problems disappear or that things always turn out the way we would like them, for very often they don't. But we succeed in managing ourselves, our reactions, our emotions, our decisions. And that really is success.

It is when we can say to God, 'I am nothing, I know nothing. Guide me', that we attain the spiritual poverty that enriches. That's when we start acting on his wisdom, not our own; with his power, not ours. After that situations begin to change that we thought never could. We find ourselves contributing positively to their improvement. And where in the past we had thought of just giving up, we discover a new hopefulness that makes us want to do more for ourselves and for others.

Poverty of spirit doesn't change the story of our life but it does change the way it is told and affects its outcome. When we read our tale back into the story of Jesus, matching our need for God with his spiritual poverty before the Father, the two stories begin to merge, they become one. The result is the amazing discovery that we are happy. And more – we find that this happiness remains as a permanent condition even when all the things that go wrong around us tell us we *should* be feeling something else. And that is what Jesus meant when he described poverty's reward as heaven itself.

38

Joyful Mourning

The second beatitude is the strangest thing imaginable (Mt 5:14): 'Blessed are those who mourn'! A contradiction, surely? Or some cryptic clue for a crossword. But it was Jesus who said it, and therefore it is true. Of course it depends on what one is mourning. Some people lament the passing of an opportunity to get rich quick, even when it involves dishonesty. Some bewail the fact that they have been caught out in their devious ways and can no longer exploit others safely.

But the blessed that Christ was referring to are those who deplore the things that go on today that are not right, and who are disturbed enough by them to make their protest felt.

St Paul was one of these. In the Corinthian community there was considerable immorality even though the people concerned were baptized Christians. In one case a man was living with his step-mother in what was acknowledged as an incestuous relationship. Paul was not only troubled about the situation in itself. He was absolutely appalled that so many others tolerated it. If no one speaks out against such things, he argued, the whole community will become corrupt!

In a series of letters (more than the two we are left with today) he made his feelings very plain. So much so that he upset those who read his words. Not a bad thing to happen, he explained later when the situation had improved: 'Even if I made you sorry with my letter, I do not regret it... because you were grieved into repenting; for you felt a godly grief so that you suffered no loss. For godly grief produces a repentance that leads to salvation' (2 Cor 7:8-10).

Those letters brought the Christians of Corinth to their senses. A protest was registered that made people see the error of their ways and change. The fact that they lived in a pagan city in pagan times was no excuse. As members of Christ they were supposed to be following the way of the gospel.

And similarly with us today. We live in a climate which is becoming more and more secular. Paul's teaching still offers a standard to judge our behaviour by. Had he kept silent neither we nor the ancient Corinthians would have had a voice to remind us of what we know to be true. He was one of Christ's blessed because he cared about what was going on.

All of us who are baptized are called to speak up when something is not right. If we don't it will only get worse. But to do so we first have to be sensitive to the tragic distortion of sin, to feel the sadness of it all, and to be concerned enough to take action. That's what it means to mourn. To care deeply enough to speak out.

It's not always easy to stand up and disagree with what you see. But it is not impossible either. To point out to a young person who is lax about his faith, 'It's not right to miss Mass', or, 'It's not right to cheat and steal', or, 'It's not right to have sex outside marriage', is quite a simple statement to make.

You may think it won't make any difference, but it will. Maybe not right then, but later. Maybe you won't know that it had an effect, but that doesn't mean it won't. Once the truth is spoken simply, clearly and sincerely it always has an effect. And the effect will begin with you. It will make you aware that you have an obligation to practise what you preach. And it will bring you the happiness of trying to help others find their happiness in God.

39

The Strength to be Gentle

'Blessed are the meek, for they shall inherit the earth.' So runs the third beatitude (Mt 5:5). Not, Blessed are the weak! There is a world of difference between weakness and meekness. The Jerusalem Bible translates this beatitude as 'gentleness'. And St Francis de Sales once remarked, rightly, that gentleness is real strength.

In fact you have to be strong to be gentle. Any coward can throw his weight about, bully others less his size, insist on his own way, walk over others till he gets it. But only one with strength of character knows that strong-arm tactics get you nowhere. You may attain what you want in the short term, but by alienating everybody in the process you lose all eventually.

People respond to the way they are treated. Behave courteously and they will cooperate, acknowledge their dignity and rights, and they will respect yours. More than that, the gentle are appreciated in themselves. It is a very attractive quality in a human being. It is one that gains friends without trying.

To the gentle is promised the earth. And the sun and the moon and the stars, we might add, for their nature inspires generosity. But Jesus did not mean that precisely (although it happens to be true). By the earth he meant one's self. The gentle inherit self-possession. Self-control.

According to the Genesis story mankind was made from the earth, the clay of the ground to which we all return. But this clay is subject to Adam's sin. Though moulded in the image of God, it can drag us down to the mud again.

Only the breath of the Spirit which the Creator breathed into the clay can raise it up to the dignity of its human worth. That spirit was the Spirit of God's gentleness. Those who possess it possess the divine image in the flesh – in other words, Christ. And that is why others seek them out, try to know them better, like them easily.

The main reason is that you can trust people who are in control of themselves. You know what to expect, you know they are stable, you know that with them you can relax. They are not liable to jump down your throat, to seek confrontation, to be one thing one moment but something else the next. Even when they disagree with you they can express themselves without belittling you.

In a crisis they do not react. They act. They seem to know what to do. They are not deflected by considerations of their own welfare or convenience. All that has been worked out beforehand by their disciplined attitude to themselves. They are free to give themselves to the needs at hand.

The freedom of the meek is enviable! They avoid so much of the hassle and bother that get most of us down. It is clearly a special grace, a special beatitude that they receive, one that makes life so much easier not only for them but for us as well.

Of all Christ's qualities it was this that marked him out most clearly as God and man; and through this one that he drew so many to himself and to the Father.

40

A Faith that Seeks Justice

'Blessed are those who hunger and thirst for righteousness, for they shall be satisfied' (Mt5:6). To hunger and thirst literally means to be unable to think of anything except food and drink. If you are starving you cannot sleep, you cannot work or concentrate or apply yourself to a hobby or read or watch television. Bread and potatoes become an obsession. Water or tea or coffee become a fixation. And that is what Jesus said happens to those whose appetite for righteousness is as great as ours is for breakfast or dinner or supper.

What was this 'righteousness' that he was talking about? How could it possibly compete with hamburgers and fries and salad? Righteousness simply means, 'That which is right' and good and proper and just. Perfect righteousness is the will of God in himself by which he governs his creation, the world and those who dwell in it. To hunger for this righteousness is to share in God's own hunger for justice and to be unable to rest – as he is unable to rest – until it is achieved.

If I do not put in the work for the money I earn, that is not right. If I take away another's good name, that is not right either. If I am unfaithful to my spouse and break my marriage vows, that is not just. If I insult my neighbour because I have lost my temper with him, that is injustice again. And if I can go to bed at night and rest without putting these things to rights, or at least without intending to do so as soon as possible, then I am not among those whom Jesus called blessed in his kingdom.

God's desire for justice where we are concerned was so

strong that he sent his Son to be crucified so we might be restored to justice in his sight. Even though it was we who sinned and not he. Knowing this, how then could I be content to wrong someone – whether deliberately or by accident – and pretend that it didn't really matter? How could I present myself at Mass to worship God without trying to mend what I had broken?

The reward that Christ promises for those who do care about justice is that 'they shall be satisfied'. The only bread that satisfies this hunger is the Bread of Life, the Eucharist. It is the inheritance of those who have worked for it by practising justice in their own lives. To receive the Eucharist and not practise justice is to make a nonsense of religion.

On the other hand, whoever is sincere in his conscience, whoever makes restitution for what he has done wrong, whoever tries to conduct his life according to the standard of the gospel, will find in the Eucharist a food that strengthens his resolve. If the hunger is there, this nourishment will satisfy it and help him make the changes that are necessary to do what is right by God. Such a person is indeed blessed, worthy of the justice he will joyfully receive at the heavenly banquet where God himself is both the host and the food.

41

The Double Blessing of Mercy

here is no quality in the human being that makes him more like God than mercy. For mercy is of the essence of God. As the old proverb says, 'To err is human, to forgive divine'.

Or as Shakespeare puts it, even more eloquently:

It is an attribute to God himself;
And earthly power doth then show likest God's
When mercy seasons justice.

When we forgive another's offence for mercy's sake, God himself becomes present in us, for Mercy is God's other name.

Such forgiveness brings a double blessing, as the Bard of Avon also wisely remarked in that passage. It blesses the one pardoned; but it also blesses the one who pardons. It is a win-all-round situation: nobody loses. If you have ever had to forgive you will know this to be true. The feeling that follows the acceptance of an apology is a good feeling. It creates a warm kind of glow inside you, whereas to withhold reconciliation spreads winter frost over your heart; it leaves you cold and chilblained.

The blessing, however, that Jesus promised to those who forgive is much, much more than a good feeling. It is the assurance of the Father's compassion when they themselves are in need of forgiveness. 'Blessed are the merciful,' he affirmed, 'for they shall obtain mercy' (Mt 5:7).

In teaching the disciples to pray Jesus showed the link

135

between pardoning and being pardoned: '*Forgive us our trespasses as we forgive those who trespass against us*'. In other words, God will not be outdone in generosity by us. Anything we overlook of another's fault will merit God's dismissal of our faults at the end of time. Indeed, the greater the debt we cancel now, the greater will be the debts cancelled against us then.

Some offences however are very difficult to forgive and forget. The hurts they cause can be a burden heavier than we know how to manage. And that is precisely why Jesus urged us to drop them quickly and completely. Resentment is far too dangerous to hold on to. The bigger it is, the more it is likely to crush you. If it turns to hatred it will certainly destroy you, and then you will be twice a victim: first of the one who hurt you, and then of yourself.

Sometimes we may feel that if we forgive we are simply giving in. But letting go is different from giving in. To let something go is to be free of it. When we let go of bitterness we distance ourselves from the wrong that was done to us. It remains with the one who did it, not with us. It becomes his responsibility, not ours. Now we can begin to live life again unencumbered, without having to drag someone else's problems after us on top of our own.

To see it in this way is indeed a mercy. *Voilà!* Already Jesus' promise has come true!

42

The Best Gift of All

'Blessed are the pure in heart, for they shall see God' (Mt 5:8).

To the pure in heart Christ promised the best gift of all – the vision of God himself. And not just after death, but right now. Those whose hearts are pure see God all the time, no matter where they are or whom they are with. They recognize him in every circumstance, in every thing that happens, good or bad, and in each person they meet. Theirs is the old Celtic prayer:

God be in my eyes and in my seeing,
in my ears and in my hearing;
God be in my mind and in my thinking;
God be in my heart and in my loving.

Because they make this prayer their sincere desire, it is always answered.

To see God in everything like this is to have him in one's heart first. It is as if Christ and the Father gaze upon the world they made together through our vision of it. They see it through our seeing. And because it is still a very beautiful creation despite man's sin they rejoice in it again and again in us.

God loves the world he made and the people who dwell in it. When anyone loves as he loves, they don't notice the flaws. Or if they do, they tend to overlook them. The pure in heart are men and women who see the beauty as God sees it and are so impressed that they miss the imperfection.

What is this purity that Christ spoke of? It is freedom

from cynicism which is really the child of despair. Cynics are people who never see any good in any one. They criticise youth right across the board even though hosts of young people are generous with their time for the poor and underprivileged. They grumble about public servants though a lot of good work is done in this field every day. They malign the Church and everyone in it, disregarding the fact that many Christians are quietly working out their salvation as best they can. Beneath the icy sarcasm and vicious negativism is a failure of faith. They simply do not believe that good is stronger than evil, that love has already risen from the dead. Their hearts are sullied with clouds and darkness and night.

The pure are people with real faith. They know that goodness has already won the victory over the nightmares of the dark. It is not that they are blind to the challenges to faith – they see these only too clearly. But because their faith is in God and not in anything else, they are not the victims of illusions as others are. Their world does not crumble when things go wrong or fail to turn out as they expected.

They know that God is in the unexpected, turning all to the good for those who trust him. Even if they have to wait to see how, they do not doubt that he will because he has promised it and has done it before. They see God even when he is absent!

And that is why they will see him for ever in the life to come. He will be no stranger to them, as they will be no strangers to him. Whoever has seen God in this world will certainly see him in the next because their heart is purified already. Having caught a glimpse of his glory as it were in a mirror darkly, they know the value of the gift they have received and will never rest content until they are looking at him directly, face to face.

43

No Peace without Parley

'Blessed are the peacemakers', Jesus declared, not just the peacelovers! 'For they shall be called sons of God.' Everyone loves peace but not everyone is prepared to do what makes for peace. The few who *are* prepared are indeed blessed because they care enough to take the tough action that peace demands.

You have to be tough with yourself when, for example, you have had a row at home. The fault may not have been entirely yours but to restore harmony you may well have to offer an apology. It takes two to make a row. To acknowledge one's part in it, even if one is more sinned against than sinning, requires humility. And that is tough, especially when one feels offended. But that is the price of making peace. One has to put one's feelings in one's pocket and forget about grievances in order to re-build bridges. Those who do so are children of their heavenly Father, for that is what he did when we offended him. And so, like Father, like son!

But peace is not just the absence of rows. It is a way of living so that rows do not arise in the first place. Bad feeling and quarrels happen only when people forget about the rights of others, their dignity, their need of love. When husbands and wives care about each other they don't ignore these things. They make each other's happiness their main concern.

The same with parents and children. If they really love one another they don't treat one another shabbily. They will go out of their way to show appreciation, to be helpful, to act kindly. That's what peace-making is. Getting in quickly before problems arise, anticipating friction and taking steps to avoid it.

With the best will in the world, of course, war will break out between the best of friends, the closest family members. At times people slip up, do the wrong thing, say the insensitive word that they wish they hadn't. In such cases the peacemaker will wisely let it go.

There is a certain ten per cent in all relationships to which we should turn a blind eye. People are not perfect and it is a generous thing to make allowance for that. It is unrealistic to expect those we live with to be saints and angels. To find the saint in them you have to accept the devil too. That is what we would wish them to do for us, as indeed they often do.

As well as humility and tolerance, the makers of peace will need courage: the toughest quality of all. Courage to challenge another person when we know they are in the wrong. This is not the same as wilful criticism or nagging. It is something entirely positive. It is the ability to approach gently and firmly about a matter that is wrong and cannot continue.

Maybe a child has been stealing or acting deceitfully. Or a wife has been overspending. Or a husband has been staying away from the home too much, drinking with his mates or working too hard. These things need to be addressed if family life is not to fall apart. When they are not discussed they simply get worse and it becomes too late to talk.

Most people hate confrontations and so they leave it. 'Maybe things will improve,' they console themselves; 'perhaps I'll only make matters worse'. This is why courage is needed. There is no peace without parley. To take one's courage in hand when one is fearful is a sign not only that one *loves* peace but that one is a peace-builder. When the motivation for facing a difficulty is precisely this, one will find fear no obstacle.

Christ never allowed fear to prevent him from tackling

the thorny situation. As God's Son he believed that his Father would complete the efforts for peace that he began. Those who share his belief share with him too in his Sonship. They are loved by God as much as Jesus himself was loved, and will reign with Christ one day in the Father's house. There they themselves will enjoy the fullness of peace they worked so hard in this life to achieve.

The Price of Integrity

lessed are those who are persecuted for righteousness sake, for theirs is the kingdom of heaven' (Mt 5:10). When the writer of Matthew's Gospel penned these words of Jesus the early Christian communities must have been greatly heartened. For they were severely persecuted for their faith nearly everywhere. In Rome, for instance, the Colosseum was drenched with the blood of the martyrs who were thrown to the lions, tortured, beheaded and burned. Very often they received no support from their families who were pagan non-believers and did not understand them.

Why would anyone want to go to their death simply for a religious creed? The fact is they did not want to, but if that was the price for freedom of conscience they felt they had no alternative.

The only comfort they had were the words of Jesus: 'Blessed are those who are persecuted.' The point was repeated again and again through Matthew's Gospel. 'If anyone loses his life for my sake, he will find it' (16:25); 'If anyone would come after me, let him deny himself, take up his cross and follow me' (16:24); 'Do not fear those who can kill the body but cannot kill the soul' (10:28); 'He who does not take his cross and follow me is not worthy of me' (10:38).

It was all the comfort they needed. On the basis of such encouragement those early believers were able to face whatever opposition came their way. And ever since Christians have found strength through the gospel to stand up for what is right. Every age has had its martyrs as we in Ireland know only too well from our memory of the Penal days.

But the persecution that is happening today is much more subtle than it was before. If fire and sword could not break the spirit of Christians in the past, material prosperity, permissiveness and religious indifference are doing their best to break our spirit now.

It is a very hard thing to stand up and be different when everybody else seems to have abandoned morality for example. Sometimes to do so will invite personal hostility. Not the physical kind of yesteryear but much worse: the snide remark, the cold shoulder, the outright ridicule to one's face or the snigger behind one's back. When you are called old-fashioned because you still hold on to standards that are right, or are put down as out-of-touch simply because you do not run with the pack, that is persecution.

Who wants to be made to feel an outsider? Who likes to be unpopular, different, eccentric? Yet there are people today who are prepared to put up with this if that is the price they have to pay for integrity. They are the stronger among us, the fully mature.

At the end of the day people who run with the pack will disappear with the pack. They will never amount to anything, they will make no impact. But those who stand on their convictions will change the world. Christ has promised it will be so. To them will be given the kingdom of heaven, the term the gospel gives to the new world slowly emerging through history that will be the only society to survive when the present age has run its course.